Girls use sex to get love,
Boys use love to get sex.

~ Maria Gsell ~

Dollar's Kreative Writing Studio

Think -- Kreate -- Repeat

This book was produced by Dollar's Kreative Writing Studio

This is Why You Not Married:

The 4 Women that Can't & The 3 Men that Won't

Photography by @spexphoto

Exterior design by Dollar's Kreative Writing Studio

Printed in the United States of America

ISBN 1947289527

This is Why You Not Married...

The 4 Women that Can't

&

The 3 Men that Won't

By: Esque Dollar, M.Ed.

Acknowledgements

Special Thanks to all of my social media followers and fans who keep me motivated with their comments, likes, and love.

The 14 Khronickles of Konfrontation,
Zeta Chi, and all the members our Noble Klan:
Kappa Alpha Psi Fraternity Inc. – "Achievement."

The Wolf Pack, 305 PACK LIFE.

Red, my love, my wife, my buddy, for supporting anything I do. Life without you would not be much of a life at all.

Dedication

To all the lives I ruined, hearts I have broken, and people I disappointed in order to learn everything in this book. I apologize, and I thank you.

Table of Contents

The Philosophies

"Marriage is not about meeting the right person, it's about becoming the right person."

~ Unknown ~

~ The 4 Play ~

It's a question as old as man itself, "How does one find love and marriage?" We are in the year 2017, and yet we're still making attempts at trying to help one another find that "happily ever after." There are websites, apps, and even courses out there designed to help with romance, and now there's my book. Trust me, I know there are already a bunch of self-help books out there that "AREN'T" being read. However, like all people with a vision...I believe I have a new take on love, relationships, and marriage that's worth your time.

So Esque...why write another one? Well, the first reason is because reading something is deeper than hearing it, or even seeing it in a video. When you read something, you attach your own visuals. Things that come from your imagination. This makes the connection with the words more meaningful, and more powerful. The second reason is because, like most humans, deep down inside I am a hopeless romantic who believes that love is in all of us, and without it, we will remain incomplete and unfulfilled. I want everyone to experience the ultimate high that I have reached. It is a travesty to go through this life never having experienced true love. And because of that belief, I truly feel that it is my duty to aid those who are struggling at finding it. Especially, helping them from the perspective of a man.

Most of these books are written by women, and usually for women. A little one-sided if I do say so myself. It's almost as if folk feel like men aren't interested in love, or learning how to "properly" secure it. Neither of which are true. Us men want and enjoy love just as much as women do. Most of us just aren't man enough to admit it. However, I am sure a large number of men will read this book...they just might not let anyone know that they're reading it...if you know what I am saying. One day we will get back to the days of men being proud to be romantic, being proud of having a one true love, proud to scream from the mountain tops, "This is my woman, and I love her!"

Additionally, I have a problem with men who feel the need to always call out the issues with women, while letting guys run free to continue the ignorance that some of us have done for generations. A man will never know what it's like to be a woman, so while it is perfectly fine to speculate and offer suggestions from a man's point-of-view, a man's area of expertise should be in that of the behavior and mindset of men. If you are man enough to point out what's wrong with women, then be even more of a man, and stand in front of your fellow-men and say, "Y'all been acting like some assholes, and it's time to do better."

The Game

The rules of the world are simple. You are either the hunter, or you are being hunted. You are either the predator or the prey. The rules one should follow depend upon which role you're playing. Like it or not women, you all are the prey. Men are the hunters. This means that the rules for each are going to be different. There are going to be things done that don't seem fair, and that's because we are not equal. Men and women cannot and do not have the same role in this game. However, even though it seems unfair for the ladies, there is something cool about it: their position.

Even though the ladies are the prey, they are the ones who decide whether or not the hunter gets to enjoy his prize. So, men go through all this stuff to track down and capture a woman, only to hope and pray that she allows him to have her. Interesting isn't it. Therefore, women, do not be so upset that it sometimes seems like all the blame is put on you all, that's because women are the ones with the power. And to whom much is given, much is expected. But I ain't saying nothing you don't already know, right?

For some, the information in this book will be an eye opener. For others, this will be the 97th time you've been told this. In either case, let this be the time that you do something about it. Progress never happens for those who continue to do things the way they have always done them.

With that being said, there is no need for a prolonged intro. The point of this book is simple. I want to provide some logical explanations for men and women on why they have yet to walk down the aisle to say, "I do." Also, I want to provide some "Changes" that should be considered in this process, and finally...add a few ways for going about making those improvements. But before we get started, I want to describe how the book is organized.

The Layout

I organized the book so that people don't necessarily have to read it in its entirety. They can skip to the sections that they feel pertain to them by reading the table of contents. However, there is no harm in reading the sections that may not speak directly to your life. Maybe you will be able to help out that friend that doesn't read, and doesn't understand why they are constantly repeating the same situations over and over again.

I believe marriage to be a 2-part system that requires two people thinking a certain way, and because of that, I will address men and women separately for most of the book. On the other hand, there are a few topics that I address and I do not separate them on a gender basis. For the women, this book is about why a man hasn't asked you to marry him yet. For the men, it's about why haven't you asked anyone to marry you yet. For my LGBT community, get in where you fit in.

I have broken single women into 4 categories:

- The T.H.O.T.
- Ms. Goodie Two-Shoes
- The Ratchet
- Ms. Independent

I have broken unmarried men down into 3 categories:

- The Playa
- The Free Man
- Mr. Comfortable

While each type of person has their own unique qualities, I will address the issues with each type that may be preventing them from holy matrimony. I will also offer some strategies for improvement that will assist in each becoming better versions of themselves because let's face it, who likes a person that points out all the negatives and doesn't offer any advice? No one likes that guy.

With the aforementioned groups of men and women I am sure that I have covered every type of unmarried person there is. This way, everyone will walk away from this book with a better understanding of why they have yet to wed, what are the things they need to change in order to get closer to a marriage, and what may be going on in the minds of those whom they are trying to attract.

The other topics that I will address separately from the individual genders are things that I consider to cross gender lines, but are also preventing the establishment of a healthy, long-term commitment. Some of them are:

- Side-Pieces
- Cuddy Buddies
- The Low-Key Crew

Pause

In case you didn't read my first book, let me break this down for you. I occasionally go off on tangents that may, or may not be relative to what's being discussed. I separate those tangents by saying...

Pause

And when I am done rambling I end it with...

Unpause

You can skip over them if you like and not miss a beat, or you can read them. If you get lost while reading them then go back and read the previous sentence and then skip over the pause. It will make perfect sense.

The pause gives you a better understanding of me as a person, and the way I think. I apologize for those of you that find them distracting, but I promise you that they are worth reading.

Think Like You

One of the lessons from Sun Tzu's legendary book, **_The Art of War_**, is that one must know their enemy. Let's replace the word enemy for prey, and say that in the dating game, one must know their prey. I think that is what Steve Harvey was trying to do with his book. His goal was to provide some insight for women into the minds of men. Whether or not he did a good job is up for debate, but what cannot be argued is that he proved many women would be interested in knowing how the minds of men work when it comes to relationships. I hope to take it one step further by providing insight into the opposite sex, as well as insight into the self, and some principles to use.

The reason is this. While you may be able to think like a man and act like a lady, you first need to master how to think like a lady, before you can even act like one. Plus, not all men and women are the same, and not all men and women are at the same point in their lives. With this book, I am trying to reach different people at different stages in their lives, and with different personalities, and show them how they can find love from those who they would like to get it from. Because the fact is while we all want love, we don't want it from just any old person.

CHAPTER – 1

WOMEN

Being the Kappa Man/Gentleman that I am, it is only right that I start with the ladies. Plus, the book is about trying to get hitched, and typically it's the ladies that are usually the ones who want to get married first.

Pause

I am generalizing here. You will see a lot of that throughout this book. If you feel like it doesn't apply to you, that's fine.

No one can lie to you like you.

Unpause

And the ladies are the ones that men get on one knee in front of. And we cannot dismiss the fact that the ladies are the ones who get to flaunt the big rock on their finger to post on social media with that lame #isaidyes hashtag. And don't forget they get all the attention from the dress. And etc...

So let's get to it then.

Single ladies, why aren't y'all married yet? It is a great question that one could spend hundreds of pages trying to answer, but I won't. I will get straight to the point. In order to do that, I must first break the ladies down into a few different categories, because not all women are the same.

Yes, it is true. Not all women are the same. On the other hand, women aren't that different. Which is why I was able to separate the ladies into only 4 different types of women.

What I did was this, I analyzed all the characteristics of women. Then, I broke them down into categories based on traits that affect a relationship the most. The more I worked through my chart, the more I was able to merge some traits, and separate others. In the end, I wound up with 4 distinctly separate categories that jumped off the page and made it easy to place all of the little nuances and traits under these 4 major ones. Finally, I either came up with or utilized some of the stereotypes out there to create titles for these unique types of ladies so that I could get everyone's attention.

Each category has inherent traits that will attract people to them. I will explain those first. It is always good to start with the positive stuff. After we discuss the traits that are making them great, we will address the things that are making them single, and unable to get a husband. I'm not going to try and balance it out, if it's more bad than good, then it is what it is. Be a big girl and accept the bitter with the sweet.

I am pretty sure that every single woman will be able to find herself inside one of these sections.

Pause

Let me be clearer. You may find a little bit of yourself in several sections, however one will/should stick out more than the others. So, don't just read the titles and be like,

"Girl he ain't talking bout me anywhere in this book."

Give each description a chance, at least read the first page. I know for certain that a mirror reflection of you will pop up somewhere. If not, then we know why you not married; because you're perfect!☺

Unpause

As you go through the different ladies I describe, try to have an open mind and leave your defensive mechanism in the off position. We can never grow if we are not open to criticism. We will never become the person we want to be if we are not honest with the man (or in this case) the woman in the mirror.

For those of you who are that much in denial regarding how you see yourself, keep this in mind. While you may not think you fit into any of these 4 classes, more than likely other people are seeing you as one of them, and that is all that matters. You've heard it before, perception is reality. As a result of that logic, it doesn't matter how nice you think you are, if the people you are trying to attract find you as aggravating as a puppy with a squeaky toy, then my dear, you are as aggravating as a puppy with a squeaky toy.

Pause

I love dogs. Shout outs to all the dog owners, and puppy lovers in the building. Shout outs go to my 3 dogs: Rajah, Rocky, and Roxy.

Unpause

Remember the purpose of this book ladies...for all of you women it is to learn some possible explanations for why a man hasn't asked you to marry him yet. Whether you want one to or not, the fact that no one, or no one that you would say yes to, hasn't even asked you should bother you a little bit. I know it would sure as hell bother me if I was you.

In my first book, **30 b4 30**, one of the stories is about my first time at a gay club. In the story I mentioned how I started to "feel some type of way" because no one hit on me while I was there. I mean, I consider myself to be a pretty attractive guy, so the fact that I wasn't getting any inviting looks, free drinks, or dance offers started to get to me. Well, if you consider yourself to be a pretty awesome woman, and no one has inquired about making you their permanent partner, then maybe you ain't as great as you think you are.

And with that, let me introduce to you, our first lady.

The
T.H.O.T.

That	Hoe	Over	There

O therwise known as Slut, Whore, Skank, Tramp, Animal, Jumpoff, Loosey Goosey, Promiscuous girl, Easy, Buss it Baby, and I am sure there are more names that I could bore you with, but I think the dead horse has taken enough of a beating. We will move on.

Everyone knows a THOT. She may be your sister, your mother, your best friend, your reflection, but like it or not, there is a THOT in your life somewhere. And you love her for the hoe that she is. And you feel bad for her because you know the odds of her finding a husband are slim.

Pause

I learned something that blew me away (no pun intended) while watching a porno documentary. All of the former porn stars started their interview with a short story about how they got into the industry. I was floored at the number of women who said they got into it because they like having sex. Not to say that I didn't know women enjoyed sex because I did, but we often think of women who become porn actresses, or strippers as women that can't, or couldn't do anything else.

We don't think of them as people who just have a career doing what they like to do. A lot of them spoke about how much FUN it was, and how they ENJOY getting some regularly, while also getting PAID for it. #happy

This made me look at them differently. If a man can earn a living because he was blessed to be 6' 7" tall and play a sport, like basketball...then, what's wrong with a woman who was blessed with a pretty face and an attractive shape earning a living doing porn or stripping? I see them as being one in the same, especially if she genuinely enjoys it, and is not forced to do it. Ain't finding what makes you happy and just going out there and doing it the point of all this?!? We can't praise the athletes, but condemn the strippers. That seems very hypocritical.

Unpause

The old saying goes something like this, "You can't turn a hoe into a house wife." Well, that is not true. Furthermore, in the lyrics of the rapper TI:

"They say that you can't
turn a hoe into a house wife.
Well listen shawty,
maybe I don't want a house wife."

Now, that says a mouth full in favor of the THOT. Pun intended.

There are men out there who don't want the traditional idea of a house wife. On the other hand, for those men who do want a "normal" house wife, and contrary to what women think, men would much rather start with a hoe and work from there, instead of trying to turn a house wife into a hoe. I will elucidate.

What They Like

I am sure there's a gang of you ladies out there that are super curious about this because you wanna know why is it that all the Jumpoffs seem to always have a man, but you can't find one. Here is where I will blow your mind.

THOTS are usually very fun people. They are the chicks that we say are, "down for whatever." No, that doesn't only pertain to sex. It also pertains to having fun. THOTS are never completely alone because men like being around fun girls.

When I was single and party time came, I would reach out to the girls that I knew were down for whatever. The ones that I knew wouldn't care what club or bar we ended up at. The ones that didn't always take 2 to 3 hours to get dressed. The ones that didn't care if we smoked weed and drunk Hennessey, or ate fruit and drunk water. The ladies that I could call and have a conversation like this with:

"What's up sweetie?"

"Hey Mr. Sexy Man."

"You got plans tonight?"

"No, not at the moment."

"Alright, I'll be there in 20 minutes to come scoop you."

"I'll be ready in 15 ;)"

These are the nights men dream about. The carefree nights. Those times where it's just you and a down to earth girl who wants to have a good time. Does it usually end up in hot, steamy, sex? Well, Duh. But that is not the point. Well, that's not totally the point.

Actually, that is the next point. The fact that, as a man, you can hang out with a chick, and not have to worry about whether you're going to get any or not, makes the night more fun. Men wanna fuck, I know girls do too, but men wanna fuck at the end of every night. At the end of every date. So I, as a man, wanna hang out with the THOT because I can focus on having a good time, since smashing at the end of the night is a given. I call it... Pussy Peace of Mind.

Men like to know where we stand with a woman. With the THOT, we always know where we stand. We stand wherever the hell we want to.

Pause

And if we want to, we can be like Theodis Ealey, and we can "Stand Up in It."
Shout out to DJ HiTech.

Unpause

Ease of vaginal access is very important to a man looking to settle down. The last thing a married man wants to have to do is fight for pussy. The thought process of a man is this, "If I gotta work this hard for some ass, then I could have stayed single." The THOT gets upgraded to a girlfriend for this reason alone. It might sound simple, and that's because it is. Men ain't that difficult at all. We want to fuck, to be fed, and to have fun. Anything else is extra.

Why No Ring

The reason why a man won't wife a THOT is not because she's a THOT. The problem with "wifing" a hoe is that everyone knows she's a hoe, except her. And that's a deal breaker.

Think about all your tramp female friends. How many of them actually think they hoes? Most smelly people don't know just how bad they smell. And to make matters worse, we, their so-called friends, often times let them walk around smelling rank out of consideration for their feelings. For example, how many of you have told your THOTing friend that she's a THOT? Not in a joking manner, but in a serious way. Like, sat her down and said something to the tune of...

"Keisha, (that's the first THOT name that came to mind) you know I love you right. You my girl, and we been friends for a long time. So, you know everything I say to you is out of love, right?"

"Yeah girl. We sistas. Tell me anything."

"Well. You's a hoe, and everyone know you a hoe but you. And I need you to get yo hoe tendencies under control so someone will marry you and get you out yo mama house. Now I know we hitting the club tonight so I want you to turn up and have fun cuz tomorrow we going to church and we gone get you prayed for. We gone ask pastor to remove that hoeing spirit outta you, and pray that God send you a good man, child."

I know we think of hoes as women that have slept with a large number of men, and I don't agree with that definition. I know women in all four categories who have slept with what most would consider a large number of men. I see the THOT as someone who everyone knows their business, that is what makes it a bad thing, and why a man won't marry her.

No man really wants an inexperienced woman. Let me repeat that. No MAN! So, a 31-year-old guy who is looking for the 1, wants her to come with some sexual experience. Whether it be that she has slept with 5, 10, or 25 different guys, a real man doesn't care. As long as she will pass all the STD tests with flying colors, her "body count" is irrelevant.

Pause

Body count is the contemporary term for the number of sexual partners that a person has had. Ladies, any man that asks you for your body count is lame as shit, probably insecure as hell, and you need to tell him a lie, and enjoy your free dinner. Afterwards, you block his ass and never talk to him again. A real man is not interested in the number of men you have had. All he cares about is if you can rock his world when the lights go out. The number of men you had to go through in order to learn how to do that, a real man doesn't care, and he salutes all the hard work your exes did.

Unpause

The issue that men have is when they know people who you've slept with. That's a very tough pill to swallow. For example, I once dated this chick that I was really into. We were kicking it for a while, and she had some male friends that I also knew. They had been friends since high school, where as I met them in college. One day she told me that she had slept with two of them before. (No, not at the same time) Initially, it didn't bother me. However, the more I started to like her, the more it started to bother me. I forgot to mention that one was a godfather to her son, which meant that he would somehow always be around.

Every time I thought about marrying her I imagined those guys being at, or in the wedding. I couldn't do it. On my wedding day, there can NOT be another man who slept with my soon to be wife within 100 miles of the ceremony Got Dammit.

While we know we are not the only one you've ever slept with, no man wants a constant reminder of someone who has been with our woman. We are not built to handle that. Maybe once in a blue moon, but not on a regular basis.

Likewise, no guy wants to be the only person in the room that doesn't know his girl has slept with every other guy in the room. Men are full of pride, and nothing fills us with more pride than having a woman to call our own. This means that a woman should not put a man in a situation to look like the town fool. Let me know before we get to the class reunion that you smashed most of the basketball team during high school. I won't hold it against you, and I will know why everyone is looking at me like I got 2 heads. If I know why, then I can handle it, or choose to stay home.

In the cases where children are involved, and co-parenting is taking place, my hat goes off to those men. I know it is not easy to always be reminded that this guy once repeatedly let loose in your current girlfriend or wife, but you make it work for the sake of the children, and for that, you should be commended.

Ms.
Goody Two-Shoes

Otherwise known as...well, there really isn't another name for her; except maybe Susie Homemaker? We usually think of this one by her personality. She's the good girl. The conservative girl. She is usually a "really nice person." Ms. Goody Two-Shoes (GTS) is the girl who the dudes probably hung out with in high school in order to get closer to her freaky friend from the previous section.

She's the one that people think will be first in her group to get married. However, she often finds herself in relationships that don't last and ends up 35 and never married, or 35 and divorced, sometimes more than once. She is the one that makes you feel uncomfortable to say curse words around, and the one that leaves the club early, assuming she even shows up at all.

What They Like

Like I stated in the beginning, GTS is a really pleasant girl with really good qualities that will attract, and could potentially keep a man. First of all, she is domesticated with all the traits of the old school/traditional wife. She cooks. She cleans. She makes lunches. She washes and folds clothes. And she does it all with a big smile on her face. Men like stuff like that.

Coming home to a hot meal fresh off the stove after a hard day's work in the trap, or at the office, is always a good thing. The feeling of a warm towel on your body, that's fresh out the dryer, when you're fresh out the shower, is a very good thing. Always having a clean place that you can invite people over to is a very, very, good thing. Those are all good things that men will appreciate when they're looking for a wife. All of the old-fashioned character traits that men "believe" their future wife should have. Unfortunately, these are the qualities you won't learn about unless you give her a chance.

Another quality that is often associated with GTS is her "motherly" aura. Men like this because they are considering the type of mother she will be to their children. When a man is ready to settle down, motherly traits are a matter of the utmost importance, and a woman needs to display that she would be the ideal mother for his children. Men will consider you to be a strong candidate for wifey with traits like that. Now, for those mama's boys out there, they fall quick for GTS for this reason. So, she needs to be weary of them.

Pause

No one likes a Mama's Boy. I wonder if there is anything more unattractive to a woman than a dude that's a Mama's Boy. Women already have to compete with other women for a man's attention and affection. The last thing they wanna do is have to compete with a woman who they can't get rid of. #MOMS
Have fun with those guys.

Unpause

Why No Ring

This is the girl who a man's mother will probably tell him he needs to look for. Which is sad because a guy who respects his mother's opinion will give GTS a chance. Sadly, some will take that chance all the way to wedding bells. I think you get the point.

The sad thing about this part of book is that there is really nothing "wrong" with Good girls per say. However, let me tell you what's wrong with GTS in the form of a story.

When I was around 29 there was a co-worker of mine who was interested in me. She was Ms. Goody Two-Shoes to the T. She had a nice shape, slim, smart, and a decent face. I will admit, I was flattered that she was into me. Usually good girls like that stay far away from me, and for good reason.

We would speak whenever we saw each other at work. I would flirt and say slick comments, heavy with sexual innuendo, however she always brushed it off, never entertaining my talent for turning any conversation sexual.

Pause

A skill that I am very proud of I must say.

Unpause

We had a mutual friend that would always ask my thoughts on her. I would shrug it off and give the normal uninterested response, "She straight." I knew what the real reason was, but I didn't wanna hurt anyone's feelings, so I would just keep it moving. I do remember her and I eating at Applebee's once. The only time we ever did anything remotely close to a date.

Well, fast forward a few years, and she ended up getting a promotion and moving on to a different work site. This was a good thing because I found myself starting to avoid her. Like I said earlier, GTS is more often than not, a good person, so you feel bad turning them down. Instead, you just try to be nice and avoid that "keep it real" moment at all cost. That is...until you have no choice.

As the universe would have it, her new position required her to come to my site for a training. By this time, I had been married for a few months now, and was pretty sure that she had heard. Especially because our mutual friend was in my wedding.

As I was walking down that hall at work I saw her, and of course I was going to be cordial. There was never any bad blood or anything like that, so no reason to pretend I didn't see her. As I got closer, she recognized me and called out, "Hey Esque."

I walked towards her and started by congratulating her on the new position and we commenced to have a normal conversation. Until it took a sharp left.

"Sooooo." I could see the sharp turn coming from the way she dragged out the "O" sound. "I see you're a married man now."

I'm assuming she found out I was married from her friend, or maybe she saw some pictures on social media. Either way, this conversation now has to end as soon as possible. So I started keeping my answers short. "Yes I am."

"Well congratulations. She is very pretty."

Pause

Why do women always wanna tell us married men how attractive our wives are? As if that isn't half the reason we married them in the first place. I don't get it. Does that make y'all feel better or something? Are you trying to gage my response? Next time someone says that to me I should be like, "You a lie, she ugly as shit."

Unpause

"Thank you very much. I'll be sure to let her know you said that." My usual response to that silly statement.

Her eyes began to squint. "Tell me Mr. Dollar. Why didn't you ever give me a chance?" Oh...yeah...she really said that. Not sure what she was thinking, or why she wanted to know, but she seriously asked me.

"You want the truth, or you want me to lie to you?

"I'm serious. Like...you knew I liked you. I've always wanted to know why I never got a shot."

Seek and ye shall find. "Well...Ok...Sweetie..." In my calmest, Denzel-like voice as possible. "Nothing about you says you got good pussy."

Her facial expression said it all. Her mouth was open but nothing came out but air. After a few seconds, she said. "Wait, what do you mean by that Mr. Dollar?" And I am sure all you GTS out there are wondering the same thing, and you know I aim to please.

When a man is thinking about a woman who he would like to settle down with, which is the stage I was at when she was trying to get my attention, one of the things that we think about is "can I see myself sleeping with her for the rest of my life?" Now, you may be thinking that I never gave her a chance, which is true, I didn't. Let me ask you this, would you go inside McDonald's looking for steak, or how about salmon? No, nothing, not nowhere in any Micky D's advertising campaigns have they ever said anything about having nice juicy steak and/or succulent salmon.

(Following my analogy?)

As a woman, you are trying to attract a man, correct? (again, LGBT get in where you fit in) Something about you has to say that you can hold it down in the bedroom. It can be the way you walk, the way you flip your hair, the way you talk, the way you put food in your mouth, the gap between your legs when you wear jeans, the way you bend over to pick stuff up, the way you chew your gum, the way you answer the phone. Something about you has to say that there is some good pussy under this long conservative-ass dress.

Now, I'm not saying show everything and leave nothing to the imagination. I have said many times that I would much rather see a woman in a nice dress than naked. However, the way you wear that dress needs to do something to the people that see you in it. It's the difference between being pretty and being sexy.

Sexy is the way you carry yourself. You don't have to have the perfect shape, hair, and weight to be sexy. Sexy is a state of mind. Hell, that's why it's called sexy, it makes people think about sex. GTS usually misses out because people think like I did, ain't nobody got time for a chick that's boring in bed, or for a chick that's finna make me work extra hard for some snatch that probably is just average at best. Not when you're looking to settle down. That's the one problem a man doesn't wanna deal with because that's a huge reason for why men wanna get married in the first place, because we tired of chasing the juice box.

Another issue that men usually see with GTS is that she's clingy. It can be cute at first! But after a while, it gets annoying, and in some cases...even scary, and runs men away. But let me explain what clingy is in case some aren't sure.

Another word for clingy is smothering, bordering on stalker lever. For example, they call you 93 times a day. You know what I mean...you go out on a date with them for lunch. You drop her back off at her job at 1pm. By 1:34 she's texting you like, "What you doing?" They have trouble with giving space and allowing a brother to have free time. Being around them begins to feel more like an obligation than a desired activity, and who wants to go from one job to another one. That's when the guy reduces the amount of time he spends with her. It goes from weekly, to every other week, to once a month if that.

The sad part is that GTS won't see the writing on the wall. GTS will not let go that easy. She has the patience of Job, and is in it for the long haul. You almost have to seriously hurt her feelings to get her to give up.

The reason they're like this is because of how rare they actually have a man. During the leap year when they get one, they hold on like an ant on a kite. They can't afford to wait another 4 years for another man. That's part of the reason why she's so domesticated: She wants to keep her man home with her as often as possible, because this way she can keep an eye on her man because GTS has insecurities.

Whether it be about her weight, (GTS is usually a larger girl) or about something else, GTS is more insecure than the other girls. This is a huge part of the reason why she's so conservative. She tries to hide it inside morals and standards, but the real issue is her lack of confidence. Her fear of failure. Her trepidations with being embarrassed. This is why her man can't get her to go to the strip club with him. It's not cause she thinks it's a nasty place. It's because she feels insecure about her own body. So why would she wanna be in a place with her man where they are surrounded by women with body types that she wishes she had?

That is a major turn off for a man. Who wants to deal with the constant pity party? Men just want to have a good time without all that negative emotion. And his inability to have fun with Ms. Goody Two-Shoes will eventually be her demise.

The
Ratchet

Otherwise known as Ghetto, Hood Rat, Trailer Park, Hot Girl, Drama Queen, White Trash, Bag Lady, and Un-couthed. This lady is the one that will probably have a baby daddy or 2 or 3. The girl who'll be in a relationship for 5 years and never be introduced to her partner's parents. The girl who you invited to go club hopping, but somehow you forgot to include her in that group message about attending the play "Rent." The girl who can't distinguish a 1st row concert dress from a 1st pew church dress. The girl who her friends call when they can't find anything on TV because they know she always got some foolishness going on.

Now, don't get it twisted, this girl isn't always a broke girl. While financial status usually equates to education and culture, because there are so many different ways one can gain financial stability in today's society, that assumption is no longer as accurate as it used to be. As a result, there are a pretty large number of people with financial stability, but without the mentality that usually comes with the attaining of it. There is a term for these types of Ratchets. The old term is

Ghetto Fabulous, and the more contemporary version is Trap Queen.

These ladies suffer from a severe lack of exposure. Most don't know more than the area they grew up in, and have done little to no traveling in their life. They are who they are, and don't know any better. And there are men that like 'em like that.

What They Like

Growing up in Liberty City Miami, I've had more than my fair share of interactions with this type of woman. As a matter of fact, most of the women I saw were like that. And because of that fact, that's what I wanted. A hood girl. I wanted a girl with braids who smelled like Pump It Up hair spray.

There are several reasons why men like the Ghetto girls. One is because the guy knows that he doesn't have to extend his self too much financially in order to impress her. For example, on my first date with my wife I spent over $100 trying to impress her.

Pause

I took her to CinèBistro, which is a movie theater where you can order and be served dinner and drinks. My wife ordered a shrimp appetizer, a drink, and a steak dinner. Had I pegged my wife as a Ratchet chick, we would have gone to Denny's, Waffle House, Wendy's, or somewhere that has wings and fries. But she is really good at hiding her ghetto side. Ironically, years later she told me that she really enjoyed our first date, and was impressed, but she would have loved wings and fries even more. #gofigure

Unpause

With the Ratchets, because they don't know any better, you can get away with things that otherwise wouldn't be acceptable. So for a man, part of the attraction is in the lack of hassle, and financial ease. Another attractive aspect of the trailer park girl is how rough they can be.

Have you ever heard two hood rats have a conversation? It is quite entertaining:

"What's Up Biiiiiiiiiitch?"

"Hey girl! I was just thinking bout yo silly ass. What you been up to?"

"Child, the same ol' shit. Still waiting on Ronnie sorry ass to pay me back dat money he owe me. He think just cus I still let him come over when Trav gone that I don't want my money back, but he messing with the right one."

"He still aint give you that money girl?"

"Fuck No. But I got a trick for his ass. Let me not have my $17 by next week. See if his wife don't find out what he really be eating on his lunch break."

"YAASSsss Girl. Get his ass!"

That is quality theater! And until you hear one of these conversations live, you haven't lived. The key is this, as long as you stay on her good side, then you good, and you can just chill and get your laughs on. You don't ever wanna end up on her bad side like Ronnie.

The most important reason why guys like Ms. Ratchet is because of her propensity for loyalty. She is usually what we call a, "Ride of Die." If you get into a fight, this is the girl who you want with you. She won't run and hide, or go get the cops. She's throwing bottles, punching, kicking, biting, and scratching, and fighting with her man, or for her friends.

The Ratchets are with you if you have a job, don't have a job, lose your job, or not even looking for a job. Because of their tendency to have low standards, the things that matter to most women, such as status, and stability, don't matter that much to them. All they care about is whether you show them love or not.

It's like a type of unconditional love that others might not consider intelligent. It takes a special kind of person to stay loyal to someone that is locked away in prison. Or to stay loyal to someone that is involved in activities which are illegal, and could land you in jail. Hood girls will stand by you no matter what, as long as they feel and believe that you love them. And that is very attractive to a man, and will make some men over look the other stuff.

Why No Ring

You might be thinking that it's obvious why Ms. Ratchet is single, because she ratchet. Well, it's not because she's ratchet, it's because all she knows how to be is ratchet. There are those that play the role, and there are those who literally do not know how to be anything else. Another way to think of this issue is a concept introduced to me inside the college of education at the University of South Florida by a fabulous member of Alpha Kappa Alpha, Dr. Brenda Townsend, she called it: **Code Switching**.

Code switching usually refers to a black person's ability to switch off, or tone down their "blackness," mainly their urban vernacular, in order to better fit within a professional atmosphere.

Pause

I'm pretty sure White and Hispanic people have this problem in their culture also, I have just never heard it called code switching. So, to all my White and Latin followers, hit me up and let me know if there is a term for this. I would love to discuss it.

Unpause

Code switching is an important ability for blacks in America because it has to do with being accepted, and not being judged negatively. As a minority, like it or not, it is important to be able to get accepted into mainstream society. At the same time, it is equally important to be accepted within your own culture. This creates a situation where a person needs to be skilled at authentically behaving in two different environments. Which can be very challenging.

In the case of the Ratchets, a man will be attracted to that rough girl image, the rawness of her attitude, her loyalty, and the ease at which it is to please her. However, when it comes to making her his wife, he will have concerns with her inability to code switch, and while that may not sound like a big deal. It really, really, really is.

In a marriage, your partner is a reflection of you. This means that if you are married to a ratchet-ass chick that has no clue how to tone it down, then she will be, "so embarrassing." You can't take her to meet your family because they're going talk about her as soon as they HEAR her coming. Can't take pictures with her because she looks like she just left the club in every picture. You don't want your daughter emulating that, so there goes the idea of ever having kids with her.

Another issue with marrying a Ratchet is the possibility of her putting you in less than desirable situations. While a man is more than willing to protect and fight for his woman, no man is interested in putting his life on the line for some foolishness. Case and point.

I was once out on a date with a young lady and several of her friends. Let's place an emphasis on HER friends, several of which were married with children. Now, while they were not my friends, I had seen them a few times so we were cool. There was a point in the night where her friends were hanging out in the VIP section and we were on the dance floor.

While getting my two-step on, a seemingly drunk dude accidentally bumped into my date and spilled some of her drink. She was standing directly in front of me with her back to my front. I felt the nudge as well, but the guy kept on moving so I kept on two-stepping. However, my date stopped.

"Damm nigga! You could have said excuse me." The guy stops and turns to face her and says...

"Fuck You!"

Now, every man in the world knows what's going through my head. I'm deciding if I feel like fighting because if I get in the middle of this, then I have to be ready to throw hands. Let me break it down like this.

- If I step in and he gets slick out the mouth,
  - I gotta hit him.

- If I step in and he moves anywhere towards her,
  - I gotta hit him.

- If I step in and he says anything to me that isn't an apology, or something that sounds apologetic,
  - I gotta hit him.

So, I put my arm around her, turned her away, and began to walk with her. My date, never the one to back down from anything, let alone a human, repeats herself over me, but louder of course. The guy responds by repeating himself, but only louder. I continue to pick her up and almost carry her away.

All the way home she cusses me out, and tells me how soft I am. Screaming how no other man she dated would have done what I did. All I'm thinking is, no good woman would put me in that sort of situation. A less hood lady wouldn't have said anything to the man. I'm not saying he wouldn't have gotten a dirty look, but she would not have made a scene over something so petty as an accidental bump on a crowded dance floor.

What's depressing is that she couldn't see how her actions put us in a bad position. Plus, what did she think would happened if her friends saw us fighting in the middle of the club? Those people have families to worry about. That was totally inconsiderate of her. Furthermore, you ain't got no clue who that dude is in the club with. I tried to tell her all that, plus that fact that I have a career to worry about. She wasn't trying to hear it, and I wasn't trying to deal with her.

Those of us men who have worked very hard to get where we are, are not going to allow it to be thrown away because some dumb broad doesn't know how to act. It may not be a situation where you are about to fight in a club, it may be a situation where you are invited to a business meeting. Let's say you're a lawyer and you are invited out with the partners of the firm and their wives. This dinner could change your life. Do you feel comfortable taking Keisha's ignorant self? Once the partners see her, your promotion is a wrap. Not to mention their spouses. You know what their wives are going to be thinking, and they always have input in the big decisions. As soon as they get back in their cars all of their wives are going to say, "Did you see that woman? I surely hope you reconsider asking him to be a partner. No way can I be around that thing on the company Yacht." Flips hair.

Ms.

Independent

O therwise known as, Ms. Boss, The Diva, and Queen B. Ms. Independent is the woman who most women wanna be, but don't want to admit it. The girl who got her own, and will let you know that she can handle it. The girl who likes to say, "I don't need a man." The ambitious ladies out there who are more interested in achieving goals than establishing a relationship. This section is all about you and why yo sadity ass can't land a husband.

We all know a few Ms. Independents who've never been married, or can't keep a man. We analyze these ladies more than any of the other 3 I mentioned, because these are the ones that we look at and say, "Why wouldn't a man want her? She's got everything." True, Ms. Independent has some very attractive qualities, I will name a few of them in a bit. However, first let us clearly identify who Ms. Independent is.

There is more to being Ms. Independent than just having a few things. It is more about the attitude, and the personality that separates women who have stuff from Ms. Independent. It's about having high standards, and even higher goals. And it's the commanding attitude that attracts men to her cave.

What They Like

What's not to like? I mean people literally sing her praises. The singer/song writer Ne-Yo put it in his song like this –

"I love her cause she got her own.
She don't need mine she say leave mines alone.
There ain't nothing that's more sexy,
Than a girl who want, but don't need me"

The rapper Lil Webbie said –

"She got her own house.
Got her own cars.
2 jobs, work hard, you a bad broad"

As a hardworking man, I must admit that I agree with these two artists. It is very attractive for a woman to be financially independent. A real man will not be bothered or intimidated by this at all. On the contrary, he would admire and appreciate all the work that was done to achieve such success because a real man knows that a woman usually has to work harder than a man does to make it happen.

The type of person that a woman has to be in order to become the only female partner in her law-firm is aggressive and cutthroat, and men find those character traits attractive. Let me be more specific, men find them dead sexy.

Men wanna FUCK Ms. Independent. They want her from the back where they can bang her head against their head-board while holding her by her pony tail. They want to spread her legs from one side of the room to the other. They wanna make her scream so loud that the other Doctors at her hospital wonder how she lost her voice. Guys want that tenacity she displays in other areas of her life to manifest itself in the bedroom. We think her attitude is sexy, and for some reason, we believe that Ms. Independent likes it rough, and that's how we want to give it to her.

While we think we know what she wants, we also believe that she's difficult to acquire. See, men have this image in their heads about what an independent woman is, and what she likes. And that's because we are thinking like men. In a man's world, a man who has everything is probably not seriously interested in any 1 woman, (See "The Free Man" in chapter 2, Section 2). Following that logic, we believe that Ms. Independent isn't interested in any one man. Therefore, getting at Ms. Independent is a challenge.

It is a known fact that most men enjoy a good challenge, and no woman seems like more of a challenge than Miss Independent. We see her as a shiny trophy to mount on our mantle of mischief. Getting a woman who don't need you is hard because, she doesn't need you. This means that the normal material things men use to attract women won't do it for her. In the words of Queen Bey (Beyonce) –

"Sending me a drink ain't appeasing, believe me.
Come harder, this won't be easy,
But don't doubt yourself
Trust me you need me.
This ain't a shoulder with a chip or an ego
But what you think they all mad at me fo."

Lastly, men like Ms. Independent because we know that should something happen to us, our kids, and household will not take a major drop. For example, I have a good friend who lost his job due to things out of his control (Budget Cuts). He was out of work for 9 months, and it really bothered him because he has 2 kids. His wife was able to hold the house down. No car payments were missed. The kids still ate well. And they were still able to have a date night here and there.

Men looking to settle down will appreciate this fact. A woman that brings stuff to the table alleviates the pressure from the man. A real man will appreciate that, not take advantage of it. But, if that's all she's bringing, then she may not get any further than girlfriend.

Why No Ring

There is a reason it is Ms. Independent, and not Mrs. Independent. Ms. Independent is a classic case of the old saying, "the same thing that will make you laugh will make you cry." Because the same traits that are making her Ms. Independent, are the same traits that are keeping a man from proposing to her.

A man is king of his castle, and a man's house is his castle, and in every kingdom, there can be only 1 king. Ms. Independent is so used to running the show and being in charge that they have trouble reeling in that attitude within their relationship. A man, a real man, knows his place and understands his role as the head of the relationship. Ms. Independent has the mentality of a man, and that will not work in a marriage, because, and I quote Orlando from the Freak Show, "...she can't be the woman and the man at the same time."

A man wants a woman. Not another man. Even if we're talking about a homosexual relationship, someone must be the head, we both can't drive this car. Ms. Independent will ruin the relationship by doing too much that is outside her role in the eyes of a man. And a man don't wanna deal with that. A man, no matter how little or how much money he makes, is still a man, and he expects to be respected, and made to feel as such.

So, when a woman consistently challenges his manhood, especially without any valid reason for doing so, he will quietly bow out, or loudly curse her out. Relationships with Ms. Independent usually don't end well for that reason. Plus, Ms. Independent usually doesn't see it as her fault. They usually say things like Toni Braxton, "He wasn't man enough for me." When the truth sounds more like, you wasn't woman enough for him.

Another reason why a man won't want to wife Ms. Independent is because of her work schedule, or her being a workaholic. Men who are ready for marriage want to spend time with their future wife. Ms. Independent didn't get that house by spending her time "Netflixing and chilling." She got it by working long hours, probably more than her male co-workers.

It's difficult to establish a solid foundation in a relationship. So, imagine how hard it is when you barely get to see the other person. When a man is ready to settle down, his patience for not being able to be near his woman will be low. He will try and work with her, but if changes aren't made rather swiftly, then she will find herself back in the singles line.

One more thing that makes marrying Ms. Independent less than desirable is that she can be very fastidious. She can be the girl who, if you reached up in the sky and handed her the moon, she would say why couldn't she get a star or two.

Because she can get herself just about anything, it's genuinely hard for her to be impressed, or even appreciative. Everyone needs to feel appreciated. No one wants their efforts going unacknowledged. Ms. Independent can make a man feel like nothing he does is good enough. And that is not good.

Once a man realizes that there in no way this can go any further, he either enjoys it until he's tired of it, or he tries to improve her. Most men who are looking for a wife are willing to overlook certain things in hopes that with his help, they can be improved upon.

The brain is trained to look for the easiest route. Meaning that a man is not going to work harder than he has to. Especially if the work he's doing doesn't seem to be worth it, or valued. In business, it's called return on investment. A man has to see that all this work he's doing is going to be worth it. Why work so hard for you if he can get everything you are offering from someone else, and not work as hard? What makes you so special? And that is the question that I cannot answer for you.

CHAPTER – 2
MEN

I'm going to come right out and say it, I don't think that marriage is a natural desire for a man. I think it's a longing that develops over time, not something that we just automatically aspire for. As men, we innately want to spread our seed. Similarly, women will naturally want to carry a child: Again, I'm using generalizations here, and speaking for the majority...not the few of you. The meeting in the middle where we get married happens for different reasons. Allow me to reference a quote that men are going to agree with, and women are going to be upset with.

"Women get married for love,
Men get married for the lifestyle."

This centers around the fact that men and women are interested in marriage for 2 different reasons. When a man gets on his knee to ask a woman to marry him, he has reached a point in life where he is looking for a certain type of lifestyle; one that can only be provided through the courtship, and marriage of a woman.

Now, I don't want women thinking that their husband doesn't love them, because that is not true.

Pause

Everyone needs to understand that we love people for what they do for us. The only people that we love for no reason at all are our children. Everyone else, we love them for what they do for us. The theory of unconditional love sounds good, the practice of it, outside of most parental situations, is virtually non-existent.

Unpause

A man falls in love with a woman because of how she allows him to live. And because he knows his life wouldn't be as wonderful without her in it. Therefore, he loves you. So, while it may not happen in that fantasy type of way that most women dream about, that doesn't mean he loves you any less.

Indirectly, this answers the question for why men get married, and for how I was able to break men down into only 3 categories. Getting married is not something that most men grow up wanting to do. It is something that we are told we should do. Most men don't get married because they want to get married; they do it because they think it's the right thing to do at the time.

Take my life as an example. When I proposed to my girlfriend back in college, I was not doing it because I, through much deliberation and soul searching, had decided that she was the person that I wanted to spend my life with. I was getting ready to graduate, and since we had been together for about 2 years, I figured why not. It just seemed like the natural next step. Not the right one.

The 3 categories of men are separated on the 3 different lifestyles that a man can lead before he's concerned about getting married. I will tell you what they like about their current situation, and why getting married is not in their immediate future. Let me also state this, there is a possibility that this man may never be interested in marriage, but more than likely, we all begin to want to be a husband. But until that time comes, a man is going to do what he wants to do, and we will not be forced into a situation.

Another thing to keep in mind while reading this is that men may go from one type to the other. Meaning, depending on where he is in his life, he may not go from the single lifestyle to wanting to be in a marriage. He may very well go from one type of single guy "Mr. Comfortable," to another type "The Playa." I just don't want people thinking that this is linear.

Finally, these are the 3 types of men that will not be asking you to marry them. There are many types of men out there, however in doing my research about why a man doesn't ask a woman to marry him, I ran into these 3 reasons more so than any other. There are other types of men that will ask you to be with them for life, and treat you bad.   But these three, they just ain't asking.

And with that, allow me to introduce you to the first brother.

The Free Man

Otherwise known as the Bachelor. This is the guy that doesn't have any responsibilities, and he isn't looking for any. The Free Man is often already established, with his career, car, and living arrangements all set. This is the man that, if he was to propose, and the two of you were to start living together, all you would need to do is pack up your clothes because he has everything else. The Free Man is the most attractive man to women that are looking to become a wife. His life is prime for a good woman to come and complete it. Assuming of course, that he feels his life is incomplete.

Being The Free Man is a rare time in life. It's that time when you don't need anyone to do the things you want to do. You don't owe anyone an explication for why you do what you do. And the most important part, you don't have anyone that you're responsible for.

I got engaged right out of college so I didn't get the opportunity to become a Free Man until my ex dumped me. That was her biggest mistake in life, and the greatest thing that could have happened to me. Once she got her own place and moved out, I found myself sad, but also free. It was an interesting transition. I was unhappy with the fact that my relationship had ended, but I started to think about all the things I had wanted to do that I hadn't been able to do. I got rid of the car I had, a Honda CRV, got a convertible Mustang. Then, for the crème de la crème, I went to the rim shop for some fresh chrome 20-inch wheels, and the party started.

In the beginning, while I was having fun, I would often wonder if I should try and get her back. Not saying we didn't talk, and have that discussion, but the more and more we talked, the more I was starting to enjoy my freedom, and then, my ten-year high school reunion came. I remember The Wolf Pack pulling up in my Mustang with the top down. We walked inside and started mingling with our old high school buddies. Almost all of them had kids, were divorced, and were nowhere near as cute as they used to be. That's when the bachelor life went to a whole other stratosphere. Put it like this, there was a 10-year window from me getting dumped and me getting married. Well, let's just say that's a whole book within itself. (hint, hint)

Why He Won't

When was the last time you went on a vacation by yourself? I mean just you and the world. Coming and going and doing as you please with no one to worry about, think about, or to bother you. If this is your life on a daily basis, then why would you be interested in getting married? Marrying someone gives up that freedom.

Remember that trip to Vegas you took last year on 2 days' notice? Can't do that anymore. Remember when the guys needed a place to have John's bachelor party, and you offered up your spot. Can't do that anymore. Remember when your friend from college hit you up saying she was in town with her sister and they needed a tour guide, and a place to crash. Definitely can't do that anymore. That big screen TV you purchased the day of the Super Bowl because at the last minute you decide to have a party. Try spending 3k on a 4k without speaking to your wife first. You won't be married for long.

Marriage comes with some pretty major responsibilities. As a man, once you get married, you are now the head of a household, king of a 2,400-sq. foot, 4-3 suburban castle, with a 3-car garage full of everything except 3 cars, and an extra bedroom that's for guests that you only have over 3 times a year: Such a waste! You now have a person who depends on you, and expects things of you every day. And, as if that isn't enough pressure, once you have a child, you now have 2 people who depend on you. The more responsibilities you have the less your life belongs to you. For the guy who is unrestricted, marriage seems more like a cage than any place that's desirable.

An interesting thing about The Free Man that women will be surprised by is that he is single, and he is not a Playa. I mean, he has a girl or two that he kicks it with on somewhat of a regular basis, and he will not allow them to establish anything formal, but he is not everywhere doing anything with everyone. He is not trying to smash as many women as possible. He doesn't have time for that, and he goes out of his way to avoid drama. So, don't assume that just because he is not interested in solidifying y'alls situation that it's due to the fact that he's preoccupied with poontang. If anything, he's more worried about getting paid, progressing at his job, starting or improving his business, and enjoying his lack of restrictions.

Pause

"A man will lose a lot of money chasing women, but he will never lose women chasing money."

Unpause

The Free Man is free for a reason, because he handles his business. Which means that he works just as hard as he plays. This means that he doesn't have time for things that take him away from achieving his goals. Which means that he isn't interested in anything that will require too much mental space, pressure, or time. This means that he is not going to be in a relationship anytime soon. Which means that the ring you are dreaming about is not in your direct future.

Will He Ever

For the women that are dating a Free Man, there is hope; here is that proverbial light at the end of the tunnel. Eventually he will begin to achieve his goals, and he is going to want to share his success with someone, but not just anyone.

When the Free Man looks at his life, he is going to realize that he is surrounded by all the fruits of his labor, and he is going to want to share it with someone meaningful. While we like achieving our goals, the only thing we like more is sharing that success with people we care about. It's like if you were to the hit the Lotto, the first thing you would do is contact your BFF, or ya homie and share the good news.

Eventually, the Free Man will grow tired of spending time with meaningless people because he will start to believe that they all leeches, and are only with him for the stuff he has. No one likes to be used. In the beginning, it's no big deal because blowing the money is new and fun, but the fun dies out, and he begins to see things and people for what they really are. He will no longer want people benefiting off of his sweat and tears. He then starts to look for a woman he can enjoy his life with, and sees the value of having someone to spend time with as a good tradeoff for giving up his freedom. But it won't be just anyone. It will probably be someone that has been there throughout the building process. Someone who he feels he can trust, and would appreciate all that he has accomplished. Someone that understands him and how much he values what he's giving up to be with her.

Ladies, if you want to win the Free Man's heart, then you need to be there, not be aggravating, be useful, and be patient. Don't be needy, don't try and smother him, don't try and do too much. You don't want him to need you, you want him to want you. When he reaches out to you, be available because his time is precious and if you're always there when he looks for you, then when he looks to settle down he will probably look for you. Don't just be cute, and available though, be of some use. He needs to see that you won't halt his progress. On the contrary, he needs to realize that with you, he can get to heights that he didn't think he would achieve alone, but you must show that, not say it. The last thing you want to do is give the Free Man directions, or ultimatums. Those things never work when dealing with someone who doesn't need you.

So, play it smart, be the backbone that strong men need. Being a Free Man is tough, so if he begins to see you as a refuge from all the madness then he will begin to love you for the way you calm the storms of his life. Be that one consistent thing that he can always count on, and he will love you for that. The more and more he confides in you, the closer the two of you will become, and you will be closer to the day where he will say he doesn't want to live without you.

Mr. Comfortable

Otherwise known as Captain Common Law, or the guy that girls have been living with for the past 3 years, but he still ain't make you his fiancé or wife. The guy that says, "Why mess up what we have by getting married?" The guy that says, "Marriage ain't nothing but a piece of paper. A paper can't prove my love."

Pause

I know this is going to hit close to home for a lot of people. It's like everyone is doing the cohabitating thing, but not yet doing the marriage thing. I have even had a conversation with a woman who said that she would like to get married, but would not marry someone she hasn't lived with yet. She is asking to be with Mr. Comfortable

Unpause

Mr. Comfortable is very happy with the status quo and has zero interest in rocking the boat. He is not really the most ambitious dude: neither in relationships nor in life. He is not fond of change, and thus, is prone to having traits of a controlling person. He likes to be in charge, even if it is not in charge of much at all. The number 1 thing he is in charge of though, is the destination and travel speed of his relationships.

Ladies, those of you who are dealing with Mr. Comfortable, hear me loud and clear. It is already inherently difficult to get someone to do something that they don't want to do. Likewise, it is very tough to get someone to do something that they don't have to do. So, if we do the math and add a person who don't wanna do it, with the person who don't have to do it, we get the guy that won't be asking you to marry them anytime soon. People are inherently selfish and lazy, so while it would be good if we did certain things, most of us aren't going to do more than we have to.

Why He Won't

There is no question in this book with an easier answer than this. I will say the analogy that everyone else uses, "Why buy the cow when you can get the milk for free?" If we are already living together, having kids together, mixing money and doing everything that married couples do, then why would a man marry you? Marrying a woman is supposed to be the only way to get some of those benefits, but if I could get a paycheck, medical, dental, and vision insurance, and a retirement plan without showing up to work, do you really think I would be there? Ever? No. I would not, and neither would you. Speaking of you, you are the problem.

Mr. Comfortable is an inconsiderate monster that you created, and he will always do the minimum to keep you from complaining. You allowed him to reach this position without earning it. You paid him before he did the work. Had you held your standards, wait, let me back up...Had you had standards, and maintained them from the beginning, then you wouldn't be laying in the bed at night wondering if he will ever ask you to marry him.

Yes, you! You, the one always on Facebook and IG looking at all your friends who've only been with their dude for 7 months, but they already engaged with a wedding date. When you out with your guy and you bump into them, you must pretend to be happy when you really madder than a bih that she got a ring before you. And she know you mad, so the first thing she's going to do is shove it in your face. Now you gotta pretend to be happy for her, saying shit like, "Girl dat ice blinding me!" All the while you really just wanna punch your man in the gut for consistently making you look like...let's face it and call a spade a spade...he making you look like a fool. A got damm fool.

When you get back to the house, you wanna say something to him but who wants to be that girl who's begging for a ring? So, you say nothing, you continue doing what you been doing, praying the same prayer you been praying, and hoping that one day it will happen. I guess your pastor never said, "When you pray, you gotta move ya feet because faith without work is dead."

Will He Ever

The only way Mr. Comfortable is going to ask you to marry him is by making him uncomfortable. You're going to have to undo some of the conveniences you've allowed him to benefit from that he has never earned. The first thing you're going to have to do is tell him that you want to be married.

If you want your person to do something different or better, then you need to express that to them. You also need to explain to them how important this is, as well as why this is important to you. You gotta Keep it 100...I will talk about this later! This is not for him to respond, this is for him to listen and comprehend. Make sure he understands how big a deal this is. This should be a 10...again, we will get into this soon! If there ever was a 10 in your relationship, this will be it.

After you let him know that this is important to you, you should next ask him if there is any reason why he hasn't asked you yet. This gives him the opportunity to hang himself... I mean to explain himself. Hear what he has to say. You might find out that you may be the reason he hasn't asked. There may be a reason/issue/problem/concern that he has with you that you two have never discussed. And for whatever reason, he hasn't been man enough to bring it up. Nevertheless, don't be that person who thinks it's impossible for them to be the problem. Always start with you.

If there are some issues that he has with you, it is your job to listen. Not to rebut, but to see things from his perspective. It works both ways. There is a time to have a conversation, and there is a time to shut the fuck up and listen. Another thing. You can't tell someone how to feel, so if you think his reasons are stupid as shit, that doesn't matter. They are his reasons and you either correct the issues or move on. Yes, there has to be some compromise of course, but you can't just disregard his feelings. Remember, you the one who wants the ring. He the one not giving it to you, y'all need to meet in the middle. Once you have this conversation, a date of expectancy needs to be established.

You should give him a time table. I know that this may sound like an ultimatum, that's because it is. This could mean him leaving you, but you have to do what you never did to get what you never had. This is not the same as The Free man who is not interested in marriage. This guy is taking advantage of you. Provide him with a date that this needs to happen by or else you are moving on to look for someone who will marry you. A person cannot be so fearful of flying that they never get to land. It's obvious that you're not happy, so either you stay there unhappy, or you take a chance by taking a stance and be adult enough to see it through should this person not meet your deadline.

Pause

Don't fall for some bullshit about saving up for a ring. A man buys what he can afford because he *understands the point is to solidify y'alls relationship. You have the rest of your life to upgrade that ring. I remember my homie got his girl a $400 ring. At the time, that's all he could afford. Now she's walking around with 4 carats.*

Unpause

On the complete other hand, maybe you're just as comfortable as he is. In that case, this state of affairs may work out. There are some who really aren't interested in getting married. I never hear those same people say that they are going to be alone and not mess with anyone though. They may say that they aren't interested in marriage, but they still out here dating, some are smashing, and want everything that comes with getting married except the legal protections that go along with it. Why? I don't know. I think those people are either: (A) selfish as hell, or (B) scared as hell.

If you love someone and want to be with them, then why wouldn't you commit to them formally? I am a firm believer in putting your money where your mouth is. If you love each other then make it "for real for real." Get that guarantee. Get it in writing. Put your retirement on the line. Put your bank account on the line. Put your life on the line. Otherwise, don't claim to love someone like a husband or a wife when you ain't a husband or a wife.

The Playa

Otherwise known as a Pimp, Mac, Dog, Ladies Man, Papi Chullo, Jenga, and Papa was a Rolling Stone. Whether he has a mouth full of pearly white teeth, or he has a mouth full of gleaming bright golds, a Playa's key to success is what comes out of his mouth, and his ability to juggle multiple women "At the Same Damm Time (Future Voice)." He is ultra-confident, usually for no reason at all, and he has one goal, to conquer as many women as possible.

The Playa is the person who goes to the buffet and tastes everything. He wants it all. His appetite is usually in the quantity of women, and he doesn't really care much about the quality. As my good friend Ricki Gibbs used to say, "I've had some rusty pennies. I've had some shiny nickels. And I've had some flawless dimes."

The question that everyone usually wants to know is...Why even be a playa? Well, dudes sleep around for different reasons. The first one is the obvious one, it's a natural desire to spread the seed. Plus, sex feels good, it's fun, and is a guaranteed climax for the man. Another reason is that there are a large number of men who believe that the measure of a man is within his ability to get a woman.

When we are young males growing up, the main things we pick at each other about are whether or not you like girls, whether or not you can get girls, and whether or not you ever had a girl. Us men spend most of our youth lying about our experiences with women (while women spend theirs doing the same thing, just in the opposite direction). This is why at a young age there is pressure on a guy to sleep with a girl; it's what's expected of us from our peers: both young and old.

Pause

Those are some sad, and misguided men. The guy who cuts 2 girls in his life is no less of a man than the cat that slays 200. The number of women you slept with has no bearings on how much of a man you are.
That's just stupid.

Unpause

Because there are men who think that way, there are those Playas who are out here trying to prove their manhood through having as much sex with as many women as possible.

Pause

The definition of a man needs to be reestablished. Because of the lack of fathers inside the house, we have boys growing up to be adults with no idea of what a real man looks like. I think the single mothers out here are doing the best they can, and God bless them. However, it takes a man to teach a boy how to be a man. To show the kid the real characteristics that define a real man. The boy needs to consistently see those in action. He needs to see what his future is or at least what it should look like.

This is how a person knows if they're heading in the right direction, because the road they're on looks like the map they have in their heads. Our boys are growing up without a map. They do not have an image in their head of a man, and because of that, they do not have a solid idea of their manly destination. We need to fix this.

Men need to step up to the plate and be fathers to the kids they father. If you're going to be a playa, then that's fine with me. Play on Playa. But when it comes to being a father, you need to be more than just a dad. More than just a weekly, or monthly visitor. Every day that little boy needs to be reminded of what a man does, what a man looks like, what a man talks like, how a man handles adversity, how a man handles success, and above all, how a man treats a woman, his wife, and the mother of his child.

Unpause

This isn't a situation where eventually he will run out of women to try to conquer. A Playa will always be successful for two reasons.

1. There is an endless supply of women out there.

2. There is always a woman out there who thinks that her cookie store can change him (clearly, they need to hear about my Sex Gap theory).

So, if you're dealing with a male hoe, then you gotta know that there isn't much that you can do to get him to stop. If this is a guy who is trying to prove his manhood in this manner, then he will be lost until he realizes what really makes a man. That's not something a woman should spend her time trying to teach.

Unfortunately, the only thing a woman can do to help a man realize what makes a man is to leave him alone. If you claim you want a real man, and you're telling him that you want a real man, but you're still sleeping with him, then in his head he is a real man, or something very close to it because you keep giving him the Vicki's. Show him with your standards. You do that by showing him what you will NOT tolerate. Show him that you got a sign on yo pussy that says, REAL MEN ONLY.

Once you realize that you're not the only one, the best thing you can do is to show him that you're not like the rest of them by no longer being one of them. No one can play you if you don't sit at the table and allow them to. Not knowing that he's messing with everyone from the A-T-L to the M-I-A is one thing, but once you know, and you still decide to stay around, then you are indirectly signing up for whatever drama, fuckery, diseases, foolishness, heart break, and buffoonery that comes from consciously dealing with someone like this.

Why He Won't

For the Playa, marriage will slow him down and reduce his abilities to frolic around town. The real Playa is not the one who's cheating on his girlfriend, or stepping out on his marriage. That is someone who hasn't found himself yet. A real Playa won't box himself in like that because Playas need to come and go as freely as possible. It is very difficult to find a new piece when your girlfriend or wife is face timing you randomly throughout the day.

Pause

I wanna go back to something I just said...What I mean by, "Playa is not the one who's cheating on his girlfriend, or stepping out on his marriage. That is someone who hasn't found himself yet." This is a man who has found himself...a man who knows what he needs to be happy. This man will not settle down with a woman who won't make him happy. So, if at some point she no longer makes him happy, he will tell her. If she can't fix it then he will get rid of her. A real man doesn't have time for side pieces and cheating. We have too much work to do. Those 30 minutes with a random are 30 minutes he could spend getting closer to his goals. Real men have goals, not hoes.

Unpause

Another reason why he ain't asking is because if he were to settle down, then that would mean he would have to be faithful and only have sex with you. That's not appealing to a Playa at all, male or female. The whole point of being a Trick is to get the New New, and different as often as possible. Sleeping with only 1 person just sounds wrong to a Playa.

Pause

I need to debunk a myth. Ladies, and fellas who are about to learn something as well, I know you have heard the old saying, "Ain't no Pussy like new Pussy." Well, I got news for you, that is not true. I learned this from the comedian Lisa Lampanelli. She is the one who said something like; "...it's not about New pussy, it's about pussy that the man didn't see coming." #mindblown

What makes new pussy so good is that the man didn't see the pussy coming. It was a hope, a dream, a goal he was reaching for. It wasn't a sure thing. So, what you have to do ladies is try to make sure that your man doesn't always see the pussy coming. You gotta catch us and put it on us when we least expect it. And like I said in my YouTube video titled, "You wanna know if ya man Cheating," NO man turns down head. Likewise, no man turns down sex that he can get without doing any work.

Most of the time men have had to do the majority of the work during sex, so opportunities for us to just lay there and be satisfied are appealing, very much appreciated. If he does

*turn them down, then he cheating. So if you
sneak up on him and try to ride the dick, and he
got a problem with that, then he cheating.
Otherwise, if you can keep the sex coming from
all sorts of unpredictable angles, then you will
have a very happy, and more than likely faithful
man. Oh, and go watch the YouTube video. I
need a million views. Please and Thank You.*

Unpause

To a Playa, him asking you to marry him
would be the end of his Playa days, so while he
may actually like you and enjoy your company, he
has to want to give up the life. Why would he give
that up for you?

Will He Ever

I used to wonder if I would ever settle
down, then I heard that Uncle Luke from the 2
Live Crew was getting married. I began to think
to myself, if Uncle Luke is getting married, then
there has to be something to it. I mean Luke has
traveled the world and watched women "Pop That
Coochie" on every continent. For him to settle
down and get a wife proved to me that no matter
how many women you have, (1) you will never get
to 'em all, and (2) no number of women can
amount to a life with 1 good one.

Yes. Eventually a Playa hangs up his Pimp
hat and passes down the Pimp mug to another
young buck. Playa's hang up their cards when
they reach a point where they desire more than

just shallow experiences. When the desire for something deeper begins to grow inside them, and they realize that you can't have something deep with several people. You can think of it like someone who is hungry, but they only eat really small meals. If you only eat an apple and some carrots then you will be hungry again in five minutes. Eventually you will grow tired of not being full and go looking for a complete meal.

Pause

There are those cases where a Playa has to be slapped to reality. You know, when a Playa has yet to realize that he's old, and no longer looks like he did 20 years ago. Or when he can no longer get it up like he used to.

Unpause

Now, this may take a while. All Playas don't reach this point at the same time. Some dudes reach it after sleeping with 5 different women, some at 15. Then there are those of us that need 100 plus to even recognize that there is more to being with a woman than just sex. And then once we recognize it, we have to then decide to want it. Which can take even more time...

I remember when I first started to recognize that I wanted more. It was in college. When I use to sleep with a girl, and 10 seconds after climaxing I'm trying to think of an excuse to get out of there as fast as possible. Interactions started to become a rerun of an old movie that I had seen too many times. That was when I began to slow down. However, that didn't mean I was ready to settle down.

Ladies, this is when you want to catch a Playa. When he is not out of the game, but he is on his way out. That's the sweet spot. If you catch him too late, then some other woman will beat you to him. If you catch him too early, then he will see you as just one of the many, and want to settle down with someone relatively new. A Playa who is getting ready to pass the booty baton is looking for that girl to show him how much better life can be with only her, instead of all of them.

You have to appease to the side of life that says stability and calmness. A Playa's life is organized chaos, so you have to show him that tranquility can not only be just as satisfying, but can be better. Slowly, you will see him starting to cling more and more to you, as you just reel him in like a fish on a hook. Just remember, he has to want it first! You can't catch a fish that ain't hungry. He'll just swim by your bait like it ain't even there. Shoot, he might even nibble at it a little, but he won't bite.

Waiting for a Playa to settle down is not something that I would recommend. If you are in love with a known Playa, count your losses and go on with your life. You have no idea when he will be done with that life, and there is no time table for when his mind will change. The fastest way for Playas to change is for them to not have any women to Play, but since women can't get on the same page...

I salute the Playa and say again...

Play
On
Playa.

CHAPTER – 3

HONORABLE MENTIONS

There are several groups of people out there that didn't make either the male or female list. There is either 1 or 2 reasons for that. 1, I didn't believe this person to be only applicable to one gender. 2, I figured that this person could be a combination, or fit under one of the other headings. In any event, I still think some information on them would be beneficial to someone out there.

These people are not getting married anytime soon either, and that's the reason why they made the book. I want them to know that we know they're out there, and I want some people to realize that this may be what's holding them back. So here are a few short pages on the group that I decided to call: Honorable Mentions.

Friend-Zoners

There is absolutely nothing sadder than seeing someone who has been placed in the Friend Zone. It's the abyss we place people that we know are interested in us, and we like to keep them around, but don't plan on ever moving forward with. The reasons why we keep them around vary from person to person. Usually they provide us with something we enjoy: company, money, entertainment, etc. Both men and women are notorious for putting, and keeping people in the Zone. But women usually keep more dudes there than the other way around.

The worst thing for a woman is being alone, and having people in the Zone prevents the woman from feeling that way. She thinks of her Friend-Zoners as Minions. She talks to her minions daily, hangs out with her minions, she may even flirt with them, but the minion can never get any. They are there to do one thing: keep her from feeling lonely! And should she ever get a man, they will all be placed on a shelf for safe keeping until she needs them again. Some people know when they have been put in the Zone. There are signs, the writings on the wall, but their optimism is blinding them from the reality. So, they stay there, in the empty place, floating around in nothingness, hoping to be rescued.

Dudes don't really keep many people in the Friend Zone. We are not interested in being totally friends with a girl. If we are communicating with a chick on a regular basis then we are more inclined to be Leeches, and have Cuddy Buddies, those are coming up soon.

The only thing worse than being in the Friend Zone is not knowing you are in the Friend Zone. I feel sorry for you people. And because I'm such an amazing person, I'm going to give you a few signs that you may be in the Friend Zone.

You might be in the Zone if:

- If you have never physically touched them
- If you have never visited their house
- If you have been introduced as, "This is my friend...." or homie
- If you do all the reaching out or inviting
- If your attempts at advancing get ignored or turned into jokes
- If they tell you they're not ready

With that being said, I want to let you know that there are some people who use the Friend Zone as a way in, and they will chill there until the right moment to strike like a snake luring in a rat. This is a tactic that mostly dudes use. They play the friend roll. They get the Oscar for best Friend-Zoner. Then, on that day you got too drunk, or that day when you call them crying about the guy you really like, you wake up next to them with your panties on your head, legs open, and bra around his ankles. Got Eeemm!

So, any dude that you know for a fact you have put in the Friend Zone, and they seem a little too comfortable there, either he ain't too bright, or he playing you. Chances are, he playing you. The Zone ain't supposed to be a place of comfort. Buddy waiting for his opportunity to strike. I love meeting couples and the wife says, "We were friends for 5 years before we started dating." I laugh and say, "No. You were his friend. He was never your friend. He was just waiting." I ain't telling you what I heard. I'm telling you what I know.

Friend-Zoners usually get dismissed at some point, or they realize that they are in the dreaded Zone and they bow out gracefully. Some Zoners hang around long enough and are upgraded, either out of thirst, or change of heart. And then there are a small percentage who end up in full relationships, and ultimately marriage. This is not a recommended path, but for some, this is the only way to get a foot in the door. Do what works for you. Just know what you're doing.

Cuddy Buddies

Friends with benefits and Bootie calls are the old terms. An even older one is Splackavellie (for you folk under 30, you might wanna YouTube Pressha – Splackavellie). The Cuddy Buddy is like the Friend-Zoner with a more specific purpose. That purpose is sex, and nothing more.

This is not the section for people with morals, and for church goers who actually follow what the religion teaches them. And don't judge me but I actually support the practice of having a Cuddy Buddy or two, or three... No more than 3 at a time.

A Cuddy Buddy is beneficial if you two can keep it at this level and use it for what it is. It's about having someone that you can have sex with and there are no strings attached. We like, and need sex. Getting it can sometimes be very complicated, which usually prevents us from doing it as often as we like. Things like kids, STD's, and relationships ruin good old- fashion fucking. One thing that Cuddy Buddies are good for is preventing you from getting in relationships you don't really wanna be in.

Sometimes we get so horny that we end up smashing someone that we really shouldn't, and once you do it once, you be like fuck it, might as well keep fucking them. That thought process gets you in a situation with someone that you really didn't wanna be in. If you had a Cuddy Buddy, then you would never be that Horny. For example, if you have been holding out for Mr. Right, and you ain't had sex in 8 months, Mr. Average is going to look like Mr. Amazing. Now, because you are blinded by lack of action, you end up with a basic dude that you wouldn't have given a second date to had you not been so bone dry.

Cuddy Buddies also help you stay focused at work, or at school. If you are studying, and you need a fix, you can hit up your Cuddy Buddy, get you some really quick, then get back to work without all the emotional stuff that usually goes with sleeping with someone. She knows to come over with no panties, bend over, get this meat, then turn back around and go on with the rest of her day so that you can get back to what you was doing. Shouldn't take longer than 20 minutes or so. But...unfortunately for those of us who can handle it, it doesn't always work out that way.

No matter what they said in the beginning. No matter how much fun it seems to be. When two people lay down with each other more than once, one of them will rise with feelings. Eventually, you end up having that dreaded conversation. You know the one I'm talking about, and if you don't, then that's probably because you're the one who has started the conversation before. The 4 words no one ever wants to hear from someone they're messing with: "What are we doing?"

These words are the sign that this is about to end. Once you hear, or read these words, end it as fast as possible and don't look back. This person wants more, and they are no longer ok with the original agreement. Unless you also want more, you need to run. They are not going to change their mind. You may be able to talk them off the ledge for a little while, but it will come up again. And again, and again, and more frequently until you move forward with them, or you kill all their hopes and dreams. Whatever you decide, do it quickly.

The best way to prevent this is to let them know upfront. Remember, always Keep it 100 (I'll explain later). Let them know that this is all you want. This way, when they start getting in their feelings, and start coming at you wanting more, you refer them to the initial conversation. I vote having the first conversation via text so that you can forward them the screenshot when they say, "What are we doing?"

Send them the screenshot that reads, "So we just fucking, right? No emotions or strings attached?" Be sure to put an arrow sticker by the response they sent back that went something; "I'm bout that life." #lies

Side Pieces

I was in college when I had my first real side piece. It was a girl who I knew liked me, and I, like everyone else, enjoyed having a fan. She originally reached out to me via Facebook and eventually I gave her my number. I would text and talk to her for no other reason than to bask in the delight of being pursued, and to feed my insatiable ego.

One night my girlfriend stayed home so I went out chilling and gambling at the casino. While I was driving, my fan text me fishing. She hit me with that (what you doing?) message with the winking emoji. It had been a few months of this and I was being a 100% good boy, even though she was consistently trying to get me to cheat.

Pause

Now, when I say good boy, I don't mean I was faithful, I just hadn't done anything with this chick yet... "Yet..."

Unpause

I told her I was headed to the casino and we started texting back and forth while I was playing poker. I was at the casino for about 2 hours and all the while she was consistently messaging me. She's what I call a super texter. One of those people who respond before you can even put your phone back in your pocket. I must admit, I found that sexy...Still not sure why, but it made me feel warm and fuzzy. I imagined her doing nothing with her life but holding her phone awaiting a message from me. When I told her that I was on the way home she sent...

"You should just come by here."

"Sweetie you know I got an old lady. Why you trying to do this to yourself."

"Man what you talking bout? I can handle it."

"No you can't darling. I've been through this before. Y'all always say it ain't no big deal. Then eventually you wanna be more and shit get crazy!"

"I'm from Lauderdale, I'm a G. I promise you I ain't like that. I like you and all but I ain't trying to break up no home. I just want me a lil piece."

As if being from Broward County meant something big...

"Fuck It... Alright... you asked for it. Send me the address." My best friend always says that nothing good ever happens when a person says fuck it...

That started my official first Side Piece. I would spend the night with her. She would occasionally stay the night with me; sometimes a few minutes after my girlfriend had just left. A few times we went out together to the movies, or something low key where no one would notice us.

We often made sure we were in the same place at the same time, but never arriving together.

A Side Piece is not a Cuddy Buddie. Like I said, a Cuddy Buddie is someone you use just for sex. Also, Cuddy Buddies are between single people. A Side Piece is more than that. First of all, you can have a Side Piece, or you can be one. If you have one, then that means you're in a relationship, but you have someone else on the side. If you are one, then you are the person on the side. One more thing. Side Pieces can also be in relationships. So, if you are married and you have a Side Piece, and your Side Piece is also involved, then you are each other's Side Piece. I know. I know. Anyway...

Pause

For what it's worth, those are the best Side Pieces to have, someone that has just as much to lose as you do. I will explain more later.

Unpause

The Side Piece is someone you actually like, and in some cases probably have some real feelings for. I did. I started to genuinely develop feelings for her. However, the problem with having a Side Piece, aside from the obvious fact that you're cheating on someone, is the same problem with having a Cuddy Buddy, they rarely wanna stay in their place.

Most of all, Side Pieces have ambitions of replacing the main person. This goes for both genders.

Pause

Now, why folk would rather come behind someone else instead of getting something they could have for themselves, I no longer understand. Like, when I was young I thought sleeping with someone else's old lady was cool, something to brag about. But as I got older, I would be thinking like, "If she swallowing and kissing me, then I know she swallowing and kissing her man. So...by kissing her, did I just swallow and kiss her man too?" Shit just stop sounding attractive at that point.

Unpause

Men and women start out saying it's just going to be like this. Then as time goes on, and the two of you spend more time together, and feelings begin to grow. You begin to confide in each other more and more. You tell them all the things that your boyfriend's doing wrong, thinking that you just venting, while simultaneously thinking how great a listener they are. Then, one day they say to you what was said to me, "You know I'm better for you than she is." It never fails.

Just like with a Cuddy Buddy, this conversation is the beginning of the end of your Side Piece. No matter what happens next, you should know that they want more and they are not going to give up. The sad part is that now, you can't just kick them to the curb because there is the possibility of them ruining your life by reaching out to your main. Or posting all your business on social media. Or popping up at your house and knocking on your door 12 hours after you got engaged.

Pause

Did I tell you the story about the time when my Side Piece showed up at my door 12 hours after I got engaged wearing some shades wanting some answers? Yeah, that really happened. I handled it like the real G I was. And was still able to smash while I was engaged.

Unpause

Now...I do have a big heart, and I don't want all you cheaters and Side Pieces out there getting discouraged. Here is the good news. Just like with the Friend-Zoners, some Side Pieces are successful in their pursuit of replacing the main person. However, that is very rare. So, if you are on the sidelines, but you have a starter's mentality, just know that you have an uphill battle that doesn't always work out in your favor. Plus, if you think this person won't cheat on you the same way that they cheating now, then you dumb as a tick on an iron dog.

The best way for a side piece situation to workout positively is for it to be done between people with shit to lose. Don't have someone on the side that has everything to gain, but nothing to risk. That is a bomb waiting to happen. The absolute best scenario is to have a Side Piece that has more to lose than you do. I once had a married homie that was a car salesman at Ford. His Side Piece was married to a millionaire. Ain't no way she going to ruin her luxury life for a broke car salesman that's already on child support. She took extra precautions.

Now I'm not saying that I endorse living two different lives, I'm just saying there's somewhat of a smart way to go about. And that's all I'll say about that because I love my wife! ☺

Gold Diggers/Leeches

This may be the shortest section of the entire book because we all know what a Gold Digger is, a Leech is what I call a male Gold Digger. They work exactly the same. They are only interested in what they can get from you financially. Some are even willing to marry for the money. So, what I want to do here is to tell you how to recognize them, and sniff them out.

First thing to keep in mind is that Gold Diggers and Leeches aren't always broke. The motivation with them is not that they lack money, it's that they would just rather spend your money. Which is exactly what I want to prevent from happening.

For the men who don't want to be seen as nothing more than an ATM, you discover her Gold Digger tendencies simply by removing the money. Do free, very, very inexpensive, non-glamorous stuff for a while. Do the Waffle House, Denny's and IHOP types of restaurants. Go to Drive-in Movies. Buy her a gift from the Salvation Army. Stay in the house and do Netflix and chill, or do nothing at all. If you notice a difference in her behavior, then chances are she's a Gold Digger.

For the ladies who want to detach a Leech, it pretty much works the same way with one exception. If a man doesn't have a job, then he is automatically a Leech until further notice. And if you allow yourself to date a man without a job then you might as well have picked a Leech up off the ground and placed it on your chest so it can get as fat as possible as you lose blood. Matter of fact, get freaky with it and get a few of them. Jump in a tub full of leeches and see what happens to you because that is exactly what you're doing by choosing to date a jobless man. In a situation where your man lost his job, then that's a different story. If he's not making any effort to get one...then you have to let him know that you signed up to love a man, and a man has a job. You gotta do him like Pops on Friday, walk up to him and be like:

"Craig, you listen to me. I want you to get your ass up today, go out and look for a job. The word for today is "job." J-O-B. You hear me? Go look for a job today. I'm not kidding."

Then add this line in there.

"You no have Job, you no get job. No Hand Job. No Blow Job. And definitely the Candy Store is closed because it needs someone with a Job to open it." Gotta let him know that there are consequences to unacceptable circumstances.

One more last thing about the true money grabbers, they may recognize this and try to play the game. Plus, their patience may increase depending on how much money they think they can get from you. This means that if you are really suspicious, you may have to do this for a long period of time. Time is the only thing that sheds light on a person's true identity.

The Low-Key Crew

I was discussing the idea of this book with a good friend of mine. An older gentleman who I consider to be a wise man. He's a little over 45, and I often reach out to him to run ideas past him, or to use his services as a photographer, and a stylist.

During our conversation, I was explaining to him some of the reasons why I think men won't ask a woman to marry them. I was in the middle of explaining one of my reasons when he cut me off and said, "They don't wanna marry her because they like Dick." He also happens to be homosexual, and after our conversation took this sharp left turn, I realized I had left something out. This is not about people like my friend, this is about the people that are Low-Key Gay, the one's on the Down Low, the ones who are "Trapped" in the closet.

In the intro I said, "LGBT get in where you fit in." I wanted them to know that I'm not inconsiderate, and I believe that they can benefit from what I was about to present. At the same time, I try to stay away from things I can't speak on intellectually. So, I leaned on a few of my gay friends for this part, and this is what I got.

There are a large group of men and women who, in 2017, are still not comfortable with being openly gay. Some just disguise it as being single and not interested. Some are in heterosexual relationships. And some, so I've been told, "are out here sucking dick and going home to kiss their wife and kids." Or vice versa. Some women are out here with their Side Pieces being other women, but they are dating, involved with, or married to a man.

For my purposes, I want you to know that it is very possible that the reason why your situation may not be progressing the way you think it should, could be because your person of interest is really interested in the same thing that you are. (I hope I didn't lose anyone...) Furthermore, it is more important for you to know that, for those of you who are aware that this is the case, there is nothing you can do about it.

Ain't no vagina in the world going to make a gay man straight. Likewise, ain't no dick big enough to fuck the lesbian out of a woman. Maya Angelou said, "When someone shows you who they are believe them; the first time." You need to let people be who they want to be. If you find out this is the case, and you're no longer interested, wish them well and go on about your business. Don't be talking smack, and spreading rumors, or blaming yourself. If anything, you should blame yourself for not recognizing it sooner.

Pause

Apparently, there are signs. I didn't ask him what the signs were because he told me that would be a whole book within itself. So just keep your eyes open for things that look suspicious. And hell, if you ain't sure and you wanna know,

just ask. Say, "Baby Girl, are you a lesbian."
Either she is going to see this as a chance to
finally tell you the truth, or she is going to say
something to make you believe she isn't. It is
what it is. What you believe is all that matters.

Unpause

The other thing that I want to address stems from what I see in children. Why is it that we still make people feel uncomfortable about being who they are? We should not still have people making others feel bad about being homosexual. Who you fuck don't make me cum so I couldn't care less where another man sticks his cock. And if a gay dude tries to hit on me, which has happened once or twice, then I treat them the same way I treat a chick I ain't interested in. "I appreciate the complement, but I'm good homie."

Pause

I mean...
I'm a pretty fly ass dude, so just like a woman
can look at me, see that, and want me,
gay dudes have eyes too.

Unpause

I have had gay students in my office who are scared to tell their parents how they feel. That made me sick to my stomach. I don't care about the gender of who my child likes. As long as their spouse treats them right, and makes my child happy, then they will be my son or daughter-in-law. But if they put their hands on my child, straight or gay, they gotta see me.

I've seen homosexuality as young as middle school. Some of the kids are proud, while others are ashamed and hiding. I hear kids bullying other kids about their sexual preference. Calling them names and insults. Who teaches a child to hate like that? Parents do. That's who. The same ones that teach people to hate others based on race. And y'all need to stop!

As a black man, and I rarely say that, we really need to quit and let folks live. The way black men publicly dog homosexuals is really bad. Especially when a lot of them aren't even man enough to come out the closet themselves. Bruh, you ain't gotta lie to kick it.

INTERLUDE

"A Night with Toni"

Sometimes you do things you don't really want to. The main reason for that is almost always because someone you care about is asking you to, and that's why I find myself upset at 3am. I'm horny, and I am driving four girls back to their hotel, and I ain't fucking any of them.

The guy in the 3rd row seat is a really good friend of mine and he asked me to help with his attempt to show the bitch in the front a good time for her 30th birthday. DJ is his name. He really likes this girl and wanted to try to impress her and show her someone cares about her. His way of doing that was to book a VIP room at a club with a bottle of Red Berry Ciroc for her and some of her friends. So, DJ told her they would meet at the hotel she booked for her and her girls, and he would pick them up so they all could ride together. I'm assuming the ride part is obviously where I came into the equation.

He drives a Camry, and I have a Suburban. Plus, he is sort of lame so I just think he wanted someone to help him out. I guess it's cool. I can play wing man. I booked the club and then drove to the hotel where I met DJ. The girls were out eating so we ended waiting about 10 minutes for them to get to the hotel.

Now, I will give him some credit, the birthday girl is attractive. She is like a mini Nicki Minaj. By mini I mean she has everything Nicki has just in smaller proportions. The 3 friends were ok. One was married so X her out. The other one looks a lot like Jill Scott. She is natural with her hair to the back in an afro puff. I think that look is cute but it doesn't say anything sexual to me, which was all I'm thinking about right now. The other girl is over my weight limit, sooooo yeah...

Fast forward to now. The birthday girl is in the front seat drunk outta her mind. She has asked me where are we going about 4 times, and I'm sure she will ask again in about 22 seconds. I had a little bit to drink but not enough to deal with her antics.

She is looking around the truck for someone to listen to her now, I guess she noticed that I'm increasing the volume on my radio. "Am I drunk?" she asked anyone who would dare listen. Did she wait for an answer? No. "I ain't drunk. I have never been drunk before. I don't get drunk." Which sounds exactly like what a drunk mother fucker would say. "It's tacky for a girl to be drunk in public. No. No. No. I'm not drunk. I'm fine." After about 2 more minutes of that, the frustration inside me had built up and I decided to voice my opinion. Mind you, I don't know any of these broads, and it is clear to me that if I get any vaginal activity that it will not come from any of the vaginas currently occupying my vehicle. With that in mind, I really couldn't care less what I say right now. So I stopped my truck in the middle of the road and turned towards Birthday Nicki and let her have it.

"Look man..." I started. My voice is aggressive, but not to scare, just to get her attention and make sure she understands my words are to be taken seriously. Plus, I have a smile on my face, well, more like a sly smirk. "Yo ASS is drunk and you need to accept that shit. You 30, ain't nothing wrong with being drunk. Embrace it, feel it. Live a little, I mean shit, YOLO. You are around friends who care about you and wouldn't let anything happen to you. So yes. You are drunk. And if you stopped messing with punk ass niggas, you wouldn't be so ashamed of being drunk, and you would be thinking bout how you can get some dick for your birthday." While I was talking she was looking at me dead in my eyes as if she wanted to mount me right there and now.

When I was done, all her friends were looking at me in anticipation for her response. I wonder what DJ was thinking as he sat in the back like a child trying to listen in on mommy and daddy's conversation. I didn't give her, or anyone else, a chance to respond. "Now sit yo ass there and enjoy what's left of your birthday and listen to this great music I'm playing." I blasted Troop, All I do is Think of You. Her friends erupted in the back as soon as they heard the first note. She soon joined in. Then, I put the car in drive and kept going towards their hotel.

I'm still upset because while I know I did a good thing by helping my friend out, his bitch ass is not gonna make a move and this wet birthday cooch is gonna go to waste. I'm assuming its wet because a few minutes ago she talked about if she was married she would have fucked her husband in the elevator at the club.

I'm trying not to let my frustration be visible and I'm switching songs and hitting them with old school baby making music. Deborah Cox, Tevin Cambell, LSG, TLC, and R. Kelly. I'm in DJ mode now, only playing each song for 45 seconds. All of the sudden I feel something vibrate in my pocket. My phone hadn't rung all night so I was surprised. I looked at the radio to see what time it was...3:34 am. All the girls I know simultaneously go through my head as I try and figure out who would, could, or should be texting me. It was a picture from Toni.

Not the usual 3 am picture one would expect. It was from the bust area up. She looked so gorgeous. It is a sexy picture without being the least bit raunchy. It's almost like a work of art that is not meant to be touched, only admired from close proximity. Her hair looks nice, it's straight and hanging to her shoulder. She has on an orange top which matches that high yellow skin tone. She is smiling while wearing lip stick that seems to be the color of her shirt. I notice earrings that are hanging to her shoulder. They have what seems to be Indian feathers on them. I see a lot of women wearing ear jewelry like that now of days. Maybe it's a new fashion trend?!? Her eyebrows are perfectly arched which brings attention to the sparkle in her eye. I spend a few seconds just enjoying such a wonderful image. I'm glad I didn't run a red light. The picture has a caption that reads "Now I can't speak for ugly women but... If you don't have a chick like me on ur arm tonight, you ain't shit." I don't know what turned me on more, the picture or the caption. I love conceited women who talk a lil shit. Makes me wanna eat them alive.

So while my passengers are engulfed in singing, "I only think of you, on two occasions..." I decide to reply; this picture is making me feel a little Thomas Crownish. If you don't get the reference watch the movie, the remake not the original.

"10 points 4 u. That was funny and you are so innocently beautiful. I Like, very very nice!"

A few minutes go by and I decide to take another look at the picture. Just flat out lovely. I figured I will send her another message.

"I really like that picture"

"Well thank u. R u enjoying ur night?"

"Yea, but its bout over. You are soooooooooo pretty you know that???"

I sent her a picture of me I took earlier while inside the VIP area at the club. Her reply was on point as always.

"n u so fuking fine! Yeah. I c ya. U da boss babe!"

When that message came in I reached the hotel and was helping the ladies out of the truck and saying good byes and what not. My attention is totally on Toni at this point. I'm mentally with her, physically I'm here going through the motions. As soon as I get them out of the car and into their hotel I grab my phone and respond.

"you alive"

"lol yup"

"Where"

"im home"

"Alone"

My Toni is a married woman, so I gotta ask that question. She doesn't live with her husband right now. On her Facebook page she changed her relationship status from married to its complicated. And folk wonder why I'm still single...

"lol yeah alone"

"where r u? Waffle house"

"Nope... Headed to your house to get something
to eat :-)"
"lmfao"

She already knows what time it is.

As I pull out of the hotel I send DJ a text.

"I'm out bruh. I had fun. Good luck with ya girl.
Try n work some magic!"

"Ok man. Be safe!"

He aint gonna smell the pussy.

It's a 10-minute ride from the hotel to Toni's place. I stop at the gas station to buy some condoms and Goody powder. I don't want to get a headache in the morning, so I'm hoping that if I take it now, when I wake up I will be good. The medicine is always easy to find in a gas station, but it's like no one keeps the condoms in the same place. Once I locate them I do the usual stop and stare.

I can't speak for most men, but buying condoms always takes me a few minutes. I like to try and decide what kind of mood I'm in and use that to help me figure out which condom to buy. Unless it's some new new. New new will always get ultra-ribbed. If you wanna make a first impression, then you gotta bring the pain. Toni and I have had sex twice already so I'm trying to figure out what I want to do. I'm actually still a little irritated from earlier, so I think I will take out my frustration on Toni's pussy...Ultra Ribbed it is.

When I get back in the car I put some water in my mouth and hold it while I dump the Goody powder on top of the water. This prevents me from tasting that nastiness. After I swallow it, I crank up and head towards Toni. I'm thinking about the last time we were intimate. After it was over she came out of the bathroom with a hot rag to wipe me off and she had on this thick comfy looking red robe. It looked so soft and warm. I pull out my cell and call her.

"Hello?"

"I want you to go sit in the living room with that red robe on and nothing under it."

"Oh, so you giving instructions now?"

I totally ignore her comment.

"And make sure you unlock the door."

She is giggling like a little naughty school girl. I can tell this is making her high like Toni Braxton.

"So, you like that robe, eh?"

"Yes I do!"

"Well I will see what I can do."

"Ok."

I hang up the phone, turn up Jeezy TM 103, and head down the highway. "YYYEEeeeeeaaaaahhhhhhhhhhh," I'm saying out loud in my best Jeezy Voice.

As I parked the car I sent her my usual text...that lets women know I have arrived.

"knock knock"

When I get to the door I reach to open it, and like I requested, it is unlocked. I open the door and see all the lights are off, and there is a candle on the kitchen counter about 8 feet in front of me to the right. To the left is a staircase where I hear her laughing as she tries to tip toe down.

"I guess I was too slow. I was trying to make it back down stairs before you got here."

As Toni was talking and walking down the pitch-black stairs, her image slowly came to light via the candle on the counter. With every step, she took that rated 10 face of hers became more and more clear. I closed the door behind me, locked it, then turned to enjoy as this angel was floating towards me. She was smiling, making me feel like she was very happy to see me. I think that is why I spend time with her when given the chance.

The thing that I like about her so much is that it's always laughs and good times. She makes me feel like I'm the most important thing in the world. When I'm with her I get all of her attention and there is never any stress, negativity, or drama. Just fun and fucking. What more could a man ask for? Maybe for her not to be married. I mean I don't agree with her messing around on her husband, but it is hard to give this up. I don't get this kind of treatment anywhere else.

She completes the staircase and takes two steps towards me. She has the robe on. My face is saying Daddy like. Next, she falls into my arms as if this is where she was meant to be her entire life. She takes a deep breath, exhales, then we kiss and I say, "That is a nice robe you have there." We kiss again. Mouths closed, lips gently greeting each other. I reach my hands inside her robe and place my cold hands on her back. I know it sends a chill through her spine. But she doesn't complain. She never complains. She would deal with the pain before she did that.

"Yes, it is a nice robe, I'm glad you like. How are you doing?"

I respond, "I'm better now." Then I place my hands under her armpits to lift her up. Toni catches on fast and elevates herself to assist me. She wraps her legs around my waist. I can feel her birthday suit through my clothes. Her body is saying take me wherever you want, and do with me what you will.

When I initially called her to instruct her about the robe and couch, my goal was to eat that pussy on the couch with her legs up on the coffee table. But seeing how she didn't make it to the couch, this kitchen counter will do just fine.

As we kiss I carry her to the counter a few steps away and place her on the edge. With one hand, I have the back of her head letting her know that these are some great kisses we are sharing. With the other hand, I'm sliding the candle back making room on the counter for her body to be laid and turned into a buffet.

All talking has ceased for a few minutes now. The only sounds are body movements, moving candles, plates, and other stuff that I'm moving off this counter, along with sounds my lips are making as they leave and reenter her body's atmosphere. Once I feel as though I have made enough room, I take off my glasses and slide them across the counter. I use that as a measurement for how much room I created. They came to a stop without hitting anything so I figured I was in the clear.

I got on my tippy toes so that I could make sure my hand guided her head all the way to the surface of the table. Then slid it out from under her once she was where I wanted. The candle was about 8 inches from her head which made her face and body look serene as the light flickered behind her. I made no attempts at playing around because I reached down and gave kitty a pet and she was READY. I kissed her belly button 3 times and then went for the lower lips.

As I started sucking on kitty's lips I used my arms to spread her legs up in the air. "Feet to Jesus" as Orlando likes to say on the Freak Show. I give each pussy lip personal attention before I lick the pearl. My mouth is so full of her wetness that I let it drip from my mouth to her clitoris and through her vagina like a waterfall off the side of a mountain. As I start licking the clit I slowly allow her now shaking legs to come down and I place them on the counter like stirrups at a doctor's office.

Toni is in heaven. Her breathing is getting deeper and her moans are increasing in volume. She is reaching for my head to rub my ears. She always lets me know I'm doing something right.

Now that my hands are free, I use my right hand and slide two fingers inside of her, and they are aiming for the G-Spot. With the left I reach for her right titty to pinch and massage it along with the nipple.

"Oh D. I'm about to cum, OHHhh this feels so good." I take her words as my cue to speed up the pace of my fingers. As I finger her faster, I also start to flick the pearl faster with my tongue. I can feel the inside of the pussy quivering uncontrollably. It feels like someone is grabbing my fingers really fast. Once she is done I slow down the pace and she peels my face away from her vagina. I still kiss the entire area while putting on a condom.

Now that I'm strapped up I climb on top of her. She takes both of her hands and places them on my cheeks and pulls me in for a kiss. Her tongue enters my mouth with aggression. She is kissing me like crazy. I'm wondering if she is being turned on by the smell of her own pussy juices.

"That pussy feel good right now huh." I whisper in her ear. She starts kissing my neck and responds.

"Oh yeah, kitty feel really good right now."

After her reply, I put the dick in. She stops kissing me immediately, opens her mouth, and goes silent for the first few strokes. After a few pumps, her body has slid back across the counter so I have to move the candle so her hair doesn't catch fire and she be like Michael Jackson on the Pepsi commercial in this bitch. She notices me reaching for the candle and starts laughing.

"I didn't want you to get burned"

"Awww, ain't you sweet," and she laughs again. Then we kiss and keep on fucking. 2 minutes go by (I'm assuming it was 2, I wasn't keeping track or anything. What type of nigga does that?), and I'm thinking to myself that it is time for a new position so that I don't bust too fast. I look at the dinner table close to us and notice that she has chairs without arms. I instantly remember this girl once telling me she liked to screw her boyfriend in chairs like that cause it made her cum. Moms always said what's good for the goose is good for the gander. So I slid back and she slid right with me.

Once my feet touched the floor I put my arms under her butt and lifted her up. Since the dick was still inside of her she thought there was no need to stop the motion of her hips so she starts steadily throwing that pussy at me. I'm trying to focus on making it to this chair 3 feet away without falling, clearly she is leaving all that up to me.

I use one hand to turn the chair around and I sit in it. Realizing the position change she readjusts her body and gets comfortable. She is moving a little slower, I'm assuming that is because the dick is going a little deeper now that she is on top. I reach around and slam both of my hands against both of her ass cheeks like a cowboy trying to get his horse to move. She lets out a sexy, "UHhhh" and starts bouncing. She is about 5' 5" so her feet are on the floor which gives her leverage to really get on this dick. Now I'm the one doing a little moaning. I find myself biting her lip, which makes her go harder. I swear I hear her saying, "Yeah, I got you now nigga." I couldn't hold it any more...

"Damm this pussy good." I had to say it. She needs to know that she is putting it down. I'm squeezing them booty cheeks as if they are handles on a roller coaster ride and I'm just trying to survive. "Damm," I whisper again. I'm having trouble saying anything more than that right now. She is now taking the whole dick. Lifting herself all the way up, and then letting that so very sexy body fall, consuming everything I got. I can feel the ripples in her thighs and ass every time she pounds down. I try to regain my pimpness by saying something slick. "So you wanted some dick huh." No Response. She ain't saying shit. She is in that Michael Jordan zone right now. I'm thinking, I gotta make it last a little bit longer.

"Turn around," I said in my normal voice. I decided to buy myself a few seconds to calm down by changing positions again. However, she simply rotated while keeping the dick inside and went back to work (I thought only Trina could do that). Also, she now has something to hold on to. From this position Toni is able to brace herself with the kitchen counter. So now she really going H.A.M. My mouth is open because I want to say something but only air is coming out. She is fucking me good at this point. I know she feeling herself because she even started to slow grind. I can feel my dick going deep. It feels like there is something inside at the back of the pussy I'm touching. I'm having trouble figuring out whether this is a good or a bad thing because she's starting to let out little whelps. Not moans of pleasure, but more like groans of pain. However, she is steady riding and the groans are turning to low level screams. I think she likes it, which is motivating me to give her more.

I slowly stand up while pushing the chair back from under me and grab her hips and start thrusting from the back as hard as I could. Smack, Smack, Smack... My mid-area is slamming against her butt. Sounds like a parent slapping the hell out of they child in the middle of Publix. I give her my five best pumps and then snatch my dick out. No, I'm not cumming, I wanna fuck her on the stairs, I'm sure her husband never did that. As I guide her to the stairs as I'm kissing her on the neck from behind while maneuvering her knees, hands, and ass into position.

Her knees are on step 3 and I place her hands on step 6; I'm actually counting the steps as I gently place her hands down. She is spread out on the steps almost like someone being arrested. I kiss her back, then I kiss her booty cheeks, they look so great in this position. I have already determined that I'm going for the knock out and this is it. I lay on her so she can feel my entire body, bite her ear and softly ask, "Are you ready?"

She laughs and says, "What you got for me daddy?"

"Some good ol' fashion Jimmy Dean Sausage"

"Well I don't feel anything yet." This bitch know she be talking shit...I LOVE IT!!! Next, I reach down and stick it in slowly and as far as it can go. Then I run my hands through her hair and get a tight lil grip of it with my left hand, slap her on the ass with my right hand, take the dick out to the head of the penis, then go straight for the 4th quarter pound action.

"Oh... Shit... Yeah... AAAaaahhhhh SHit yeah!" She can't keep her mouth closed. "UUUHHH." She is letting out all sorts of sounds and each one is making me drive my dick harder and harder inside her pussy. As she begins falling forward I think to myself; Oh Hell Na...

"Don't do that, lift yo ass up and take dis dick boo." I'm back there feeling like King Kong. I'm talking big shit. She has lifted her hands off the stairs and has them on the hand rail now. It looks like she is trying to grab whatever she can.

I lean forward to kiss her on the cheek while steady stroking and she arches her head back and whispers to me "Ohhh, you all in this pussy baby." Ohh that shit turned me the fuck on. After that, I gave her everything I had left.

"Yeeaahhh I cumming," she said...I'm thinking the same thing. I can feel the orgasm climbing from my nuts and building up. I think she can tell as well because now she throwing it back...Can't give a nigga an inch I see...

I feel it about to come exploding out of my manhood, so I shove it up in her one last time and leave it in so she can feel the throbbing of my dick and what it does after I cum. Toni has her back arched now as if she has came, and is relishing the feeling of my dick just being inside her pulsating... After a minute of the laying in the pussy and letting it marinate I ask, "How are you doing sweetie?"

"I'm doing really good right now." I kiss her after she replies. We chilled on the stairs for several minutes before I walked my naked self to her couch. I think I'm just going to pass out right here. FLOP...

I hear a not so happy female voice coming from the kitchen area. "Did you just flop yo naked ass on my couch." Toni lets out as she walks toward me with the red robe on.

"Yes, I did." And with that comment I close my eyes.

A few seconds later I feel her warm body laying on top of me. It feels so soft. She kisses me a few times letting me know how satisfied she is with what has just taken place. We are naked, under her red robe, and quiet. That may have been one of the best sexual experiences of my life. Her body feels perfect on top of mine. I can feel every curve, and they just seem to fit perfectly with mine. Her skin feels like the best sheets money can buy. She is starting to caress my body with her nails and it feels extremely soothing. But all I'm thinking is, why is she married??? Am I falling for a married woman?

I hear Andre 3000 in my head, "Be cool, be cool" followed by the loud scream in the back, "ICE COLD." But I don't feel too icy right now. I feel like a little boy who just had his first kiss. My heart is warm and it feels as though it is in a place that it has always wanted to be. I'm getting goose bumps now. Toni is probably thinking they are from the way she is gliding her nails against me. And while I repeat, it is soothing, the goose bumps are coming from the thoughts I feel snowballing inside of me.

Am I falling in love? Have I already fallen? Am I in love? Is it because she fucks me good (More like GREAT to be honest)??? We have gone on 2 dates, so maybe it is possible for me to have feelings.

Wait...
What?

I realize what I just said. I'm going on dates with a married girl...

NO WAY, "Be Cool Be Cool. ICE COLD!!!"

How the hell did this go from me being upset because I didn't think I was getting any, to finding out I got some snatch on the way, to me now laying here trying to decide if I'm in love with another man's wife?

As I continue having this debate in my head, the picture she sent me earlier creeps in and I feel myself crack a little smile of admiration. She is so freakin' pretty. Blood is rushing from the top of my body down to the lower half, and I feel my dick getting hard. What am I doing? This chick has a spouse. Not a boyfriend, or some dude she fucking, but a husband...Did I mention they have kids? But no other aspect of me is trying to hear what the brain is saying. My dick has now reached full attention and I reach for her hand and she allows me to place it on my newly awakened soldier. Instantly she begins to stroke it.

She fucking does EVERYTHING RIGHT...I'm laying here trying to figure out what have I gotten myself into. I'm halfway enjoying the semi hand job she is giving me because I'm still arguing with myself about my feelings. (That sounds gay, like, I feel like I should follow that sentence up with no homo or some other disclaimer.)

"UUUUhhhhhh…" I let out as she has somehow gotten Sargent Penis in her mouth. She just has the head in her mouth and is licking the top of it in circles somewhat fast, but somehow slow. I say to myself, FUCK IT. Maybe hubby wasn't doing something right, and while I possibly have fallen for his wife, I'm definitely going to stop thinking about it and enjoy getting my dick sucked.

CHAPTER – 4

STARTING FROM THE BOTTOM

Now that you know the type of person you are, and the type of people you might be dealing with, it's time to discuss the foundations of building a solid relationship, and understanding how they work, or can work.

I'm going to present a few ideas that will assist you in understanding the tennis match that is creating a relationship. I call them "My Foundational Philosophies," and with sexual issues being the number 1, or 2, reason why people get divorced, then it should be no surprise that more than one of these ideas has to do with sex.

The Sex Gap

The sex gap is a theory that I conjured up after many sexual encounters, many sexual conversations, a few sex books, the occasional trip to the local porn store or website, and scores of conversations with my wife. The point of this theory is to help women understand why they don't view sex the same way us men do, and for men to better understand the power of the poontang.

Sex means more to women than it does to men for many different reasons. Most people think it's because women are emotional beings. There may be some logic to that, but the truth is that men are emotional as well. Men just tend to be better at hiding their emotions, and do not allow them to control their decision making as much as women do.

Most dumb men, (and most of us are pretty dumb about women) think that they have a golden cock. 50 Cent calls his the "Magic Stick." Well, some guys are right, and they can take care of laying it down. However, most men have little, to no clue, on how to truly and completely satisfy a girl.

Equally as disturbing is that I've never met a woman who didn't think her candy store couldn't change a man's life. I guess everyone is a sex god, at least in their own eyes.

This is the ultimate misunderstanding that has held women back for centuries, and why women tend to lose the sex battle. For a woman, the difference between good sex and bad sex looks like this:

Bad Dick   Good Dick

0   -   -   -   -   -   -   100

Notice how the scale's range is from 0 – 100. Seems normal right. Now let me show you what the scale for a man looks like...

Bad Pussy   Good Pussy

0   -   -   10

Notice how this scale only ranges from 0 to 10, a radical contrast from the women's. When I present this to guys, most of them shake their heads in agreement and say something like, "That sounds about right." The only guys that have a rebuttal are those who have not "lived," and who listens to an inexperienced man anyway. However, this always bothers the ladies when I show them, and I understand why.

We all would like to think that, when comparing the quality of something, there should a huge gap between horrible and amazing. Well, there is such a gap for women, just not for men. And if you really think about it, it makes sense.

What makes good pussy? I remember my wife asking me this question, and I think that's the moment when I came up with this theory. As a man, when you try to quantify quality coochie, there really aren't that many factors. Let's try and label them:

- Good Pussy is:
    - Always Wet and Ready
    - Tight
    - Easy to get to
    - The woman can handle dick
        - No matter how deep the guy goes, she doesn't complain or try to squeeze you back out with her legs
    - The girl is actively engaged
        - Providing positive feedback
            - Noises, moans, groans
        - Offering directions
        - Throwing it back/Twerking
    - Be Down for any position, and any hole
    - Oral Abilities
        - The biggest let down in my life is how few women are good at oral sex. This could be a separate chapter all by itself. But it's not that important for guys, its more about the fact that she did it, than how good she actually does it, but being good at it is always a plus!

That's it ladies. I'm sorry to be the bearer of bad news, but that's about it. There isn't much to having some good good. Really not complicated at all. Those are really the only traits that matter to a dude. And, the funny part is, most men will never have a girl who's a master of all of them. Most men won't marry the girl who's the best they ever had. Sad, but true. Now let's label the different things that make good sex for a female:

- Good Dick is:
    o Size Matters
        ▪ Size does matter, but bigger isn't always better. Some women want 5 inches, some would kill for a brother with 10.
        ▪ Thickness is a whole different conversation, and makes a difference as well.
    o Hardness
        ▪ Every erection ain't equal! Some feel like steel beams, while others feel like squishy baseball bats that kids play with.
    o Attraction
        ▪ The more attracted a girl is to a guy, the better she will enjoy it.
    o If she climaxes

- Something guy's never have to worry about because this is an automatic for us.
- Ladies, if you have sex 100 times, will you come 100 times like a man? I didn't think so.
○ Oral Abilities
  - This is really important for women because for most girls, this is the only way to guarantee they will have an orgasm. So while for guys it's exciting just to get a girl down there, for women, that's only step 1. Once he gets there, a whole different set of anxiety sets in because she doesn't know if she will cum or not because he may not know what he's doing. So stressful!
○ Tempo
  - This is about knowing how to adjust and switch between speeds, and because a woman isn't usually in control at all times, it can be a little bit of a task to get the movement you want when you want it.
○ Duration
  - Another problem men don't have to worry about.

- While this one is obvious, the truth is some chicks don't wanna be getting pounded for 30 minutes. Some are good with a solid 35 pumps. While others want 350.
- o Strength
  - Refers to the man's ability to maneuver her around the bed room and make her feel like she's with a man.
- o Sensualness (Romantic abilities)
  - Including: touch, talk, time, lighting, music, and all of the other foreplay components that illicit a sense of passion.
- o Multiple positions
- o Freakiness
  - How nasty is the guy willing to be? Fruits, syrups, toys, and all that "50 Shades"-type stuff
- o Kissing
  - I personally only kissed about 10% of the women I've slept with. Kissing isn't that important to us guys. Definitely not important when evaluating how good a girl is/was in bed.

And I'm sure that there are things that I, as a man, have left off that matters to women. However, I hope the point has been made. There is a major gap between how the sexes view good sex. This is why women are wrong when they think that what's between their legs will get a man to do things. It will never work when he can go across the street, and the drop off between you and your neighbor is borderline insignificant. You will never win that fight.

While sex is a weapon, it cannot be used to win the hearts of most men, there has to be more there than just sex. On the other hand, with it being so difficult for a woman to find an amazing sex partner, it is now clear why some women cling to certain guys, or flat out go crazy. Good dick is hard to find. So once a woman has found some, she wants to keep it because it is literally almost impossible to replace.

Fellas, something else to keep in mind regarding the sex gap is this. Chances are, you are not the best lover your wife ever had, you're the best love she ever had. (This can be a BIG difference, literally). Which means that somewhere out there in the world, is a dude who gave it to her better than you did, do, or can, and she remembers that. So as long as you out love her past, you will have nothing to worry about and she will be yours forever. But, should you slip up and forget to put that woman first, don't be surprised when Jodi starts knocking your wife into fantasy land.

Remember the quote that I got from Maria Gsell on the first page of the book:

"Girls use sex to get love,
Boys use love to get sex."

Love means more to your wife than sex, and if she married you then the sex is good enough, in conjunction with the love you provide, to satisfy her and make her happy. HOWEVER... If you begin to slip in the love department. Then that desire for the amazing sex that she use to get from someone that is not you, will start to grow inside of her. And the longer she goes without some great love to compensate, the stronger that sex desire will increase. Eventually, she will go looking for the great dick she used to get. Think about it like this. If she's going to be in a situation where she's not getting the love she wants, then she will at least get the dick she wants.

What's really depressing for men is that we really don't know where we land on her good dick scale. No one knows but her. Just because she may make you feel like you are the best, that might not be the case at all. She may just value everything else you bring to the table so much that it manifests itself when you two make love. Got you up here thinking you King Kong when in actuality you Bubbles.

With the difference between good and bad sex being so great for women, and men really not being able to know exactly where they fit on the scale, it's best to focus on loving her as best you can. You may not be able to compete with the dicks of her past. Brother, you just can't compete with genetics. What you got is what you got.

NOW, there is something for men that is equal to the female sex scale. I present to you, the Headache Scale.

Small Headache   Big Headache

1   -   -   -   -   -   100

When evaluating a woman, the last thing a man wants is a headache! However, any man who has ever dated a woman knows that she is going to be some sort of a headache; the question is, how big of a headache will she be?

The best analogy for this is that of a car. When do you buy a new car? Usually it's when the one you currently have begun to act up, and break down. I mean you love this old car. It took you to your first job. Got you through college. It's where you slept at on your 21st birthday. But when it stops running like it used to, you start to question those memories. You know, the A/C doesn't get as cold as it used to, it has broken down on you a few times, and left you stranded around town. The old car has become too much to maintain, and is now a big ass headache, so it's time to get a new one.

Let me start with this, we know the new car is going to require some type of maintenance, all cars do, but the amount of maintenance relative to the satisfaction you get from the car is what determines how much of a headache we're willing to deal with. Did you follow that ladies?

As men, we want an easy, stress-free as possible, low-aggravation type of life. This means that we want a woman who is going to keep the stress, aggravation, and difficulty level as low as possible. Hence, the phrase high-maintenance is more relative than you know!

Ever notice how when you ask a dude about a girl he likes, we often refer to her as being a, "really cool chick." Cool is easy, smooth, very little problems. The key to not being a headache is to be as low maintenance as possible. So here are some of the things that make a woman a headache:

- Don't be Needy
    - As your man, I'm here to help you, but don't be calling on me to assist all the time, especially not with stuff that we both know you could do for yourself. Initially, men love doing things for their woman, but ladies take advantage of that and then it becomes a headache. For example, I always used to say that my wife forgot how to drive and open doors when we started dating. Not to say that I have a problem with driving her around, and opening doors, but I told her once, offer to drive every now and then. This way, driving doesn't feel like something I have to

do, which in turn, turns driving intro a headache.

- Have a Life
    - We need you to have friends, a sorority, a volunteer group, book club, recreational volleyball or softball league, something that is all you and has nothing to do with us. This way, you won't always want our attention all the time.

- Know how to Leave Me Alone
    - "Absences makes the heart grow fonder" is very true. We need to miss you, and I can't miss you if you call me 10 minutes after you just left the house.

- Trust Me
    - Nothing is more aggravating, and unattractive than an insecure woman, especially when I ain't the one who broke your heart. Don't be asking me who text me all the time. Don't be asking me who am I on the phone with. Don't be asking me who that is in the back ground. It's a real headache to have to answer the same questions all the damm time. Just because all your girlfriends are getting cheated on doesn't mean that you are too. Every woman with a vagina is not after me. Have some faith in your man, until he gives you a **LEGITIMATE**

reason why you shouldn't. Plus, if you gotta be doing all that, then maybe you just need to be single until you and your voices get on the same page.

- Minimize the Crazy
  - It's a generally accepted concept that every woman is some form of crazy. Crazy is a headache, because by definition of the word crazy, it doesn't make any sense. A woman who can keep her crazy under control will be less of a headache.

It is worth noting that the more attractive you are the more of a headache you can get away with being. We live in a visual world where people like things that look nice. Men place a high value on physical appearance. I don't mind paying $700 a month for a BMW 745 because I think it's a beautiful car. Ain't no way I'm paying over $250 for a Camry. So, ladies, make sure you don't be too much of a headache, and you will be alright.

To be fair, there are a few things that men do which can be make a girl's head throb. They are not the same of course. For example, if a man is high maintenance, then he's gay... Just saying... Here are the main reasons why a man is a headache:

- Not being a good listener
  - This is the most important one. I think what happens is we work so hard to get the girl that once we got her, we don't want to work so hard anymore. So, we don't pay as much attention as we use to. I have found the best way to fix this is to pay full attention to my wife whenever she wants it. Which is all the time.

- Not having a Job
  - It's just not in a woman's DNA to have any sort of understanding for a man who doesn't work. The idea of her having to take care of a man is like a fish out of water playing basketball. Just sounds stupid.

- A Minute Man
  - It already takes a lot for a girl to get warmed up and ready for sex. Then she gotta get out of all those clothes, and then the Spanx, and before she can get a good groove, it's over. Shot out of the air before you get to cruising altitude. Guys, if you have a tendency to blow your load fast, then your tongue needs to move even faster.

The Real Them

When meeting someone and beginning the journey of matrimony, sex always ruins things. It keeps the two people from really getting to know each other in order to make the best decisions as it pertains to moving forward. The girl doesn't know if this is really him, or if he just wants some snatch. The guy wants some snatch, but he doesn't want the chick to think that sex is all he wants. And the game goes on and on. Well, this next philosophy solves that problem and allows you to get to know the real person. Here's a quick story.

Before I got married I was engaged to a cool chick from New York that I dated back when I was in college. On our very first date I drove to her school, which was across town from mine, and picked her up. Mind you, I wanted to fuck. My goal at the end of the night was to get her back to my place, eat her like a New York style pizza, and dive in like Tre Songz. So, my plan was to play it cool and wait for my moment.

When she got in the car, she put her seat belt on and turned to me and said, "Do you eat pussy." Time stopped. For 1 tenth of a second I was blown away. I remember thinking, "What kind of girl ask a nigga that on the first date?"

I gathered myself really quickly, and smoothly responded without a smile or a smirk, "Yeah, all the time." And that Kryptonite was good enough to slow this superman down. The result? I simply enjoyed my time dating her, and we didn't talk about sex again for over 2 months. To boot, it was powerful enough to keep me together with her for the next 6 years.

Looking back on that conversation, I often wondered what was so magical about her asking me that question, and what sort of impact did it have on us starting a relationship. I eventually figured it out, and now I share it with you. I call it:

"Take the Pussy off the Table"

Ladies, in order to get to know someone you have to remove sex from the equation by taking the pussy off the table. It needs to be done as soon as possible to break down the walls and facades that men have when you first meet them. This allows the man to act more natural instead trying to figure out what he needs to do so he ends up in your panties at the end of the night. If not, you end up playing the normal game of cat and mouse. There are two ways to remove sex from the equation. You fuck, do it early, and make it a part of the situation. Or you say that sex is not an option until...and with that thought, let's analyze how the cat can win.

By doing it early I mean just that. Have sex as soon as possible. This happened once with a young lady I dated. We slept together on our first date and from that point on everything was easy. We were able to get to know each other really well. Eventually we decided to go our separate ways, but we did it knowing exactly what we were getting from one another. Getting sex out of the way early saved us months of games.

Once the two of you fuck...getting sex and all the drama that can sometimes go with it are no longer an issue. Sure, he may play you to the left, and you may never hear from him again. But what did it cost you, one night? Would you instead prefer it take 6 months to find out he's a jerk? But there is something to consider, if you're the kind of person that believes sex to equal monogamy, then this option isn't for you. Commitment does not exist this early in any situation.

Pause

For the record, I'm assuming that folks out there ain't sleeping around without condoms and pills. It's 2017, if a girl is not married, and there is no medical issue, then she should be on the pill (or something like it) as well as making sure her dude, or dudes, use a condom. STD's are real. Especially KIDS. No ifs, ands, or buts about it. The last thing the world needs is another kid born to two people who don't want a kid with each other. I'm a FIRM believer in Planned Parenthood. So men, wrap that lil shit up. Ladies pop them pills like candy.

Unpause

The 2nd, and probably the most popular way, (not for me) is to say it upfront. The conversation should happen within the first two or 3 times you two speak. But certainly, by the end of the first date.

It's really simple, and shouldn't last longer than 30 seconds. Just say, "Hey, I just wanna let you know that I'm not having sex until marriage." Or you may say, "Just a heads up, I do not have sex with anyone that I'm not in a committed relationship with." However you decide to word it, the results will be the same. The guy will know that sex is off the table. He may ask why, but you don't owe him an explanation.

Two last thoughts on this. First, do not be scared of running off a good man, because this will not bother a good man at all. He will be thankful for your up-frontness, and the date will continue. The kinds of men that this will scare away are men that you don't want anyway.

Secondly, there will be some men who take this as a challenge. They will hear your words, but will disregard them and continue to pursue you as they would with any other chick. You have to show them that you mean what you say. This will be where you establish the type of woman you are. If you lose this battle, your words will mean nothing forever.

Keep it 100 (from 1)

Plain and simple, be honest. No, you can't control whether or not the other person is going to live by this same code, but you want to lead by example and set the precedent for how you will treat them. Which usually translates to how you want to be treated. I know you're trying to protect yourself, I mean no one likes getting their heart broken. But being dishonest is exactly how you end up sad and lonely. And dishonesty includes withholding information and/or feelings.

When I was dating, I would let the girls know from the jump that I'm not looking for anything serious. I'll be a gentleman, and treat you like a lady at all times, but I'm out here having fun. And when I began to look for a wife, I would let women know that a wife was what I was in search of. I learned that it's always best to be upfront with people and tell them what you want. If you want some dick. Say that shit. If you want a wife. Say that shit. If you just out here having a good time and you don't want nothing serious. Say that shit. If you're married and you looking for a Side Piece, then say that shit too.

The best thing we can do is to let a person know where we stand, what we want, and what we don't want. Once that has been communicated, then we allow them to decide on whether they want to deal with us or not. But remember, mean what you say and say what you mean.
If you tell a chick you just want a Cuddy Buddy, then don't be a stalker. If you tell a dude

you are looking for a husband, then act like you're trying to be someone's wife. Whatever it is you say you are looking for, tell them up front, and act like it. Let them know what they are getting interviewed for so that they can decide whether or not they wanna apply for that position. The only people you will scare away are those who need not apply in the first place. Moreover, tell them your standards up front.

In the beginning, do not pretend to be ok with things that you know for a fact bother you. If it won't be ok when you're married, then don't pretend its ok just because you're only dating. Before you start a real relationship with someone they need to know what's expected of them. So be specific and explicit in how you want to be treated, and what you expect them to do, and not to do.

Contrary to popular belief, you do have to teach someone how to treat you, and how to love you. Should you have to teach them everything? No. But there will be a learning curve. I once asked my homie Henry Perez at what age will he start talking to his daughter about sex. His answer was perfect, "As soon as it comes up." Take that same approach in your relationships. As things come up, state your position. Let people know where you stand at all times. This way, there are no excuses when they screw up and you go upside their head, or kick them to the side. Never let, "Why didn't you tell me?" be a viable excuse.

The last pointer I want to give regarding this is to make sure that when you speak, people know exactly how you feel. If you are at a 10, with 10 being you are pissed off to the highest level of pissitivity, then they need to know that you are at a 10. One problem with communication is that we don't always ensure that the person we are talking to understands just how important this topic is. If you are really happy about something, then you need to make sure this other person has a clear understanding of just how happy you are. Are you at a 3 happy? A 7 happy? They need to know if they did a good job, but they could do better. Or that you are the happiest you have ever been in your life.

Assigning a number to your feelings helps you as well. If you begin to scale your feelings and your issues, as well as your happiness, you will become better at dealing with your emotions because you will develop emotional perspective. I know you know some people that, with them, every issue is a 10. That is illogical, and they probably don't even know it. If they were forced to put their issues on a totem pole, then they would be forced to truly think about what's going on. Hopefully, they will realize that everything is not a big deal. Then, they will come to you appropriately. Don't scream, holler, and curse for something that's only a 4. Some people only know how to express issues in that manner, and by considering this concept, this will force them to find better, more receivable ways to express themselves based on just how big of a deal it truly is.

As for the listener, this in no way means that a 4 is not something that needs to be dealt with. Having it on a numerical scale allows for me, as the listener, to understand the sense of urgency that is needed. Is this something I need to drop everything and correct right now? Or is this something that you are just letting me know that I need to be cognizant of. Big difference between those two, and there should be a difference in how those conversations sound.

This is the only way to make sure that whoever you are talking to gets exactly where you're coming from. What is the point of having a conversation, only for the two of you to walk away from it with different conclusions? You leave thinking he gets that this issue is a 10 in your eyes, but he thinks you're just at a 5. That is clear miscommunication, and whatever issue you two were discussing will be a problem again.

Live Alone 1st

Men and women who have not lived alone for a significant amount of time, (2 years at least) are not ready for marriage. And while I really believe this to be true for both sexes, I think it matters more for a man to have this experience than a woman. Here's my logic:

1. A man that has yet to live alone has yet to prove his manhood. The very essence of being a man stems from his ability to stand on his own 2 feet. So, if a woman is looking to marry a man, then the fact that he has yet to live on his own means that he is not a man at all, and therefore unqualified to be a husband. For that reason, why would a woman agree to dedicate her life to a guy who has yet to prove that he can do the very things he's vowing to her that he will do?

You wouldn't go to a doctor that hasn't graduated medical school yet. Would you? So why would you agree to marry a man that hasn't even proven to you that he is that, A MAN. As a woman who knows her value, who comprehends all that she brings to the table, you should have a certain expectation for the man who wants to marry you. And if such a man presents himself, then there should be tangible proof that he can be all the things you need him to be, and that he claims he will be. If he needs a wife to help him to get on his feet to be a man, then congrats to his wife. She has just raised a man. Good luck with that experiment. Very few women are that thirsty.

2. I do not think that a man who has never lived alone can truly appreciate having a wife, having a partner, having a permanent supporter. Those of us men, (notice the us) who have lived alone know what it's like to be alone, to have to clean the whole house alone, cook alone, eat alone, pay bills alone etc... Those lonely nights you experience as a bachelor are where you grow into a man. Those nights where you can do whatever you want, but you choose to do nothing at all because you would rather do something with someone that has substance, instead of just having another shallow evening, are the nights that prove your maturation.

So, once we get a good woman to assist, we go above and beyond to make sure that she is appreciated, loved, and desired. Furthermore, when things get rough, we aren't so quick to shout divorce. We are more willing to work it out. Again, because we know that the single grass is not greener. Which leads me to my last point...

4. A man who has never lived alone is WWWWAAAAAAYYYYYY more likely to cheat than one who has. Now, I won't say too much here because I ain't trying to ruin people lives, but...

(Yeah, right...)

Those of us men who have lived alone have had experiences that men who haven't lived alone cannot, and will never understand until they get the opportunity to live alone. Being a single professional man with his own place is the only way for a man to learn who he is as a man, so that he can figure out what type of woman he needs to keep him happy for life.

Meeting someone, going out on a date, and having the option to take them back to your own place changes the dynamics of that date, and dating life in general. It's easy for a girl to be conservative when you have roommates...and for the record, yo Mama is a roommate too. But when she knows that you live alone, and no one will hear y'all knocking pictures off the wall, it's a little more difficult for her to implement Steve Harvey's 90-day rule.

Also, on the flip side, being a man who knows that you can do whatever you want, whenever you want is powerful. So, being on your own will help you develop the discipline needed to NOT bring every Becky, Nina, and Keisha (white, latin, black) back to your house. It will be the same self-control that will keep you from allowing Becky, Nina, and Keisha from ruining your marriage. Because being married doesn't mean that women will stop trying to talk to you.

Pause

Actually, sometimes this ring is like a magnet. It amazes me how women bash men for being dogs as if men are cheating alone. The amount of people, men and women, out there who are willing to mess around with married folk amazes me. Now, I'm all for cheating on your boyfriend and stuff like that. I mean, it's bad, but it's not that big a deal. However, when you go before all the important people in your life, not to mention your God, and you still break every promise you made, then what does that say about you? Furthermore, as the non-married person smashing the married person, or shall we call them what they are, the Side Piece, how can you be ok with having sex with someone else's husband or wife?

If they are married, then you know they are having unprotected sex. So off the bat you don't know what sorts of germs you coming behind. Second, like my homie Bishop told me, "A dude will fight you bout his girl, but a nigga will kill you about they wife." Sleeping with a married person is tantamount to courting death. What do you say if hubby comes home and catches y'all in the act? Then there are those of you who are cheating and have kids in the mix.

Nothing, and I mean nothing, ruins a child's life like having to watch their parents fight and go through a divorce. I have had countless kids in my office with tears in their eyes talking about how their parents are getting a divorce and they wish it wasn't happening. I have had 2 different kids this year crying about how they found out their dad was cheating on their mom. Kids don't understand this stuff, but they know it's bad, it hurts, and some never heal from it. So before you cheat, go to counseling, or just leave. Don't ruin someone's life because you are being selfish! Especially, don't ruin the life of these kids, they didn't ask for this.

Sorry, that was a longer tangent than normal. I guess I kind of got in my feelings a little bit.

My bad.

Unpause

I once heard an old married guy say, "I'm married, I ain't blind." Being married doesn't mean that you will no longer see attractive women. A man needs to learn how to control himself before he becomes someone's husband. That should not be something he needs to learn after the fact.

Money Ain't Equal

On Netflix, there is a documentary called the Science of Sex Appeal. (A must watch for anyone interested in this stuff beyond your own personal life!) In it they do a series of experiments to explain why we like what we like. The one about sex appeal and money stuck out to me.

To prove their theory that women are attracted to men that have money, they took photos of men and had women judge them based off of their looks alone. Some got 10's, some got 5's. Then, they performed the same experiment, however, they added names, ages, jobs, and salaries to the guy's photos. Strategically, they gave the guys with the lower physical rating the high paying jobs, and the guys with the high physical ratings got the lower paying jobs. They then took the pictures back to the streets for voting. Wouldn't you know it, all the previously thought ugly guys now became 10's because of the money they made, and the fine guys became unattractive because they were broke.

This is nothing new. I'm sure we all knew this, women like men with money. But what most women don't know is that this doesn't work both ways. Money does little to improve how attractive a woman is to a real man, if anything at all. If I show a man a picture of a picture of an attractive woman and ask him to rate her and she is a 6...giving her a job where she makes 250k a year will not change her to a 9. Men, and I mean real men, don't care about stuff like that.

Real men understand that it is our job to be the provider. It's our job to be able to deliver the necessities of life for our family. This means that, while it is nice to have a woman with a good job, the amount of money that she makes is not going to help her much in getting a man to want to spend his life with her. Now, with that being said, does that mean that dudes are out here looking to marry a basic chick? No. Nothing could be further from the truth.

Most men want a woman who is bringing something to the table. We are not looking for her to bring the table like a woman might be. We want someone that can help. In my case, I wanted a woman who, if something were to happen to me, the drop-off in lifestyle wouldn't be that big.

Well, what does this mean for the women out there? Simply this: Do not let your financial situation cause you to act as if that should impress a man. When we are evaluating a future wife, the money she brings in is not in the top 3 slots on the totem pole we use to evaluate you. It's more like sprinkles on ice cream, it's nice, but it's something that a real man will be more than willing to live without if the other character traits are there.

Chris Rock said that women won't go backwards in lifestyle, where as a man won't go backwards in sexstyle. So...if you professional women are wondering why you can't keep a man, but the broke chicks seem to always have one. Then, maybe you should ask them for some pole tricks. Give me the girls that are holding it down in the bedroom and makes $18 an hour, over the female dentist who complains about swallowing, any day of the week.

The 3 Levels of Change

No one is perfect. It is impossible for you to meet someone that doesn't have a few things that you would like them to change. You can find the happiest couple in the world, and the two people in that relationship will have a few aspects of the other person that they wish could be changed. With that being established, I created this idea to help people understand the realities of change in a relationship, and I will start with this.

You won't be able to change everything that you don't like. So, as you grow with this person and you see things you dislike, before you bring them to your spouse's attention, you need to ask yourself if this is...

1. A Change that Needs to be made
   a. If they don't change this then the relationship will not work out. I cannot be with this person unless this behavior and/or issue is completely transformed or resolved. There is no compromise here. This needs to stop and be corrected.

2. A Change that I would like to be made
   a. The behavior is not a detriment to the relationship but it needs to be changed. However, it doesn't necessarily need to be eradicated. There is a happy medium that I can live with if a few adjustments are made.

3. A Change that I would like, but Don't have to have
   a. Nothing is going to change here. I'm not even going to bring it up. This is something that I do not like at all, but I am going to grin and bear it and allow them to do them. Here is where I choose not to fight every battle.

Those are your only options when it comes to change in a relationship. And believe it or not, you will find yourself doing a lot of level 3, very little of level 2, and almost none of level 1. If you have a lot of level 1's then you either have a personal problem, or you actually don't like this person. There is no need for you to be with someone when you are trying to change every aspect of them. You just need to find you a new partner.

Another reason why the levels are important is because you may be asking someone to change something about themselves that they actually like. If that is the case then you need to chalk that up in the level 3 column. I don't know anyone that is going to change too many things that they actually like about himself or herself. The last thing you wanna do is change someone to the point where they no longer like who they are. That will turn into resentment for you and grow into a dead relationship.

I'm sure you've heard the phrase, "The Same thing that will make you laugh will make you cry." This really applies to relationships, and change. It is kind of like a weird Butterfly Effect, because for everything that you ask someone to change, there will be some residual scarring that will taint the thing that you liked about the person in the first place. For example, I can be very impulsive, and sometimes my wife says that I embarrass her and do dumb shit. I always tell her that the same impulsiveness that makes me do dumb shit is the same impulsiveness that makes me surprise her with gifts, or random dinner dates on Tuesday. Changing behavior is really changing the way a person thinks, and when you do that, there is that yin and yang affect. So be careful what you wish for, because what causes them to do things that get on your nerves is the same that causes them to do the things that you love about them.

Lastly, I want to talk about how to get change to occur. It's really simple. The bigger the incentive, the faster the change will happen. This means that you gotta give a puppy a treat when it sits or else when you say sit he will just look at you as if you had two heads.

Chances are, you're asking them to change or do something that they don't wanna do. You have to motivate them. Ladies, you may be thinking that you shouldn't have to incentivize your man to get him to do, or stop doing something. And Fellas, you're probably thinking that you shouldn't have to con your old lady to get her to fix something. You both are right, but theory and practice are rarely on the same page. It's very hard to do something you don't want to do, so if this change is really important to you, grease them up a little. Ladies, offer him something he wants, (I vote head, that always works for me) and see if that helps. Tell him you will say yes to that New TV, or to that Vegas trip, or you will think about that 3 some idea he had. Guys, offer her those red bottoms she likes, or that new Chanel purse she sent you a screenshot of. Whatever it is you have to offer them to get them to make the changes you want, just do it. It will get done faster, and you will be happier sooner, than if you continue trying it without some sort of incentive.

#thoughtprovocations

These Foundational Philosophies are things that I want you to always keep in mind as you go through your relationships, and advise your friends and family. Everything needs a solid foundation in order to be able to stand the hurricane. These theories are rooted in a mindset of preventative maintenance.

Think about it like this, would you rather do your research and homework on your next vehicle purchase before or after you buy it? It's only logical to go into this purchase with a framework of how you want things to go as well as some good rules of thumb that can save you hundreds, and in some cases thousands. My philosophies are the rules of thumb, and The Realms are the frameworks. Now, have we discussed the frameworks?? Well, I'm glad that you asked!

CHAPTER – 5

THE 5 REALMS OF RELATIONSHIPS

A key issue with people in all aspects of life is their inability to know their role and work within it. Most of us are ambitious, and therefore are always looking to progress, to do better, to be better, and to have more. We usually see this attitude on the job, and with material things, but it is extremely evident within relationships.

People don't like to think of relationships as having roles, and stages, but they do. We want them to be these limitless dreams with an infinite number of possibilities and directions. That sounds good. However, from the moment your eyes meet, the two of you have entered into a game of give and take, a power struggle if you will. Filled with rules and regulations, powers and responsibilities. And if you can learn to work within them, you will be that much closer to ensuring an outcome that is in your best interest.

I call the stages of relationships...realms. And I have created 5 of them. This chapter will make sure you understand what's going on in your relationships. Everything from the first meeting, all the way up to the wedding day. It starts with understanding the 2 most important aspects of each realm, or each relationship.

The 5 Realms

Allow me to introduce to you, the graph of the 5 realms. The great Frank Underwood said that, "Everything is about sex except sex. Sex, is about power." So, on one side of our graph you will find Power, what you can and can't do. Voltaire said that, "With great power comes great responsibility." Which is on the other side of the graph, and refers to what you have to do, or what you are expected to do.

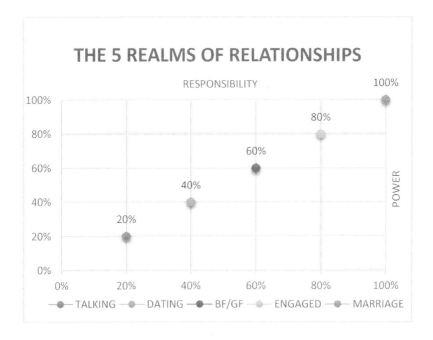

Like I said, Power refers to what you can and can't do within the relationship. It's your ability to do things like ask someone their whereabouts, go through their things, stop by their house without permission. Understanding how much power you have is vital to staying in your lane. And staying in your lane is vital to growing a positive relationship. Staying in your lane can also help prevent you from doing things you shouldn't, and allowing people to try you when they don't have the right to.

Responsibility is what you are supposed to do, and what you are expected to do in the relationship. Everybody has some list of expectations in relationships; the realms help to keep those expectations organized. It keeps them in stages, and allows for them to increase as the two of you progress. For example, someone you are talking to shouldn't expect to hear from you every day. On the flip side, someone that you are married to, better hear from you every day.

As you see from the chart, the percentages increase the closer you get to marriage, where they max out. The realms are designed to allow more things to happen the further the relationship goes. It is a system where certain things don't happen until a certain realm is reached. This allows for there to always be something to look forward to. It creates a process that has payoffs for progress.

One last note before we dive into the details, if I address something in 1 realm, it may not be addressed in the next because all powers and responsibilities carry over from realm to realm. They increase, they don't decrease. It's like a graduating scale if you will. It will make more sense when you see it. Got it? Now let's get into it.

Talking = 20%

The first realm of relationships is called talking. When you first meet someone, there is a point where it goes from platonic to something more. The two of you have just met and there exists a silent understanding that there's some potential here that you want to explore further. Talking is the beginning of that something more, its step 1. This means that y'all ain't friends.

Pause

Someone you want something more with is not your friend. Someone who would sleep with you is not your friend. I'm a firm believer that single men and women ain't, and usually can't, be just friends. Especially not if the two of you communicate on a regular basis. That means that someone likes the other, and the other just don't know it. Maybe one of you is ugly, because that would also prevent progression. Either way, you are not friends. Ladies, if you think he is your friend, seriously offer him the cookies.
If he turns into the Cookie Monster, then he ain't your friend.

Unpause

It is important that you be honest with this part. Don't let someone try and hang around as a so-called friend when they wanna do things that are beyond the friend zone. Gotta keep things within the realm they belong.

In this realm, the two of you are feeling each other out. Mainly communicating through the phone, or via the internet. You may meet up once in a blue moon, but nothing on a regular. When the two of you do hangout, it's never somewhere with a lot of people, or a lot of light. It does need to be in a public place in case you just met a psycho, but for the most part, talking happens discreetly, and on the low. It's about getting to know each other to see if there is potential for anything further. So, keep it private, don't want the wrong people seeing you with this person.

Power & Responsibility

There are no obligations/responsibilities in this realm other than the fact that I know you, and I know we are trying to get to know each other. That's what 20% is. It gets you acknowledged, and occasional communication with a possible meeting in a not too public place, nothing more. Also, talking is not exclusive. I always say a person should talk to as many people as possible. There is no harm in conversation when you are not already committed to someone else. It's called shopping around, and all the smart buyers are doing it.

As for Power, you do get to ask certain questions. For example, if the two of you haven't spoken in a while and you reach out with a text or a phone call, you have the power to ask if everything is ok. And the person you're talking to owes you an answer. Now, they don't owe you the whole truth, but something so that at least the two of you are on the same page. On the other hand, if you see this person out in public with someone else, you do not have the power to do, or say anything more than "Hi" as you continue walking. Preferably though, just don't say anything at all. Please don't text them 2 minutes later like, "I see you." That's so lame bruh.

You don't not have the power to know where they live. If you decide to link up, then you meet somewhere. Talking is not the realm where you have people picking you up from your house. You don't know them like that. Even if you chose to smash on the first meeting and get sex out the way, then you go to a hotel. A place where you can be alone to do your business, and still leave to go about your business.

-Realm Progression-

There are 3 roads that people take from here. You either place this person in the Friend-Zone, they disappear from the face of the earth, or they progress to the next realm. This means that there shouldn't be any social media posts here. Very few people should even know the two of you know each other until you decide which direction this will go. Most of the people that you will meet in life will go no further than this realm. So why have a permanent record of individuals that will soon be irrelevant to your life?

<u>Dating</u> = 40%

Once the two of you have gotten to know each other a little bit, the two of you see potential, and you want to spend more time with each other, dating is next. There is a difference between Dating, and the first realm of Talking.

Had someone else came up with this theory, then they might have merged Talking and Dating, however, I'm a private person. I don't like my business being everywhere. So, when I came up with the realms, I felt that there should be a difference between the people I don't' really know, and I don't wanna be seen with just yet. The main difference between the first two realms has to do with privacy.

Once you realize, or decide that you are really interested in this person, this is where you will have that first real conversation about, "Where is this going?" You will want to address this, and everything directly. Remember my Foundational Philosophies, I said always keep it 100, and always lead by example. What this looks like at this moment is you explaining to them how you feel, and that you wanna move forward.

If the guy is anything like me, he's going to want to know what moving forward looks like, and you should be able to tell him, and vice versa. Guys, if you are ready to move forward, then be the man and take the lead by letting the lady know where your head and heart are at. This will make her feel comfortable with opening herself up to you so that the two of you can stay on the same page.

Dating is where you can be more out in public with this person. Dating is where you begin to get to know each other on a deeper level, a more personal level, headed towards an intimate level.

Now, if you are following my strategy, then sex has already been taken off the table. Which means that either you two are fucking already, or you have set a time for when such a thing would take place. I recommended no sex without a commitment. However you decided to handle it is up to you; dating should not change the initial time frame you set for sex. Set your standard and stick to it! Do not let the fact that you're starting to like them change what you already established. He won't respect your words if he knows that he can always smooth talk you into changing your mind (and vice versa). Not a good foundation for a relationship.

-Power & Responsibility-

Now that you're dating, you are responsible for making time for this person. Not just texting, and phone calls, but dating requires more consistent, and more frequent face to face interactions. You do have the power to know where they live because at this realm you should be picking each other up from home. If you are having sex, then they may come inside and do it at the house instead of a hotel at the end of a date. But...you do NOT have the power to spend the night, pop up, or come by unannounced. After sex is over, you can chill for a little, but you gotta go at some point. Don't be trying to hang around. Kiss each other good bye and go on about your business. And again, never pop up. Please don't do that. That's a good way to get dismissed.

Dating gives you the power to be in public, but not the power or responsibility of public displays of affection. Go out, hang out, maybe even get a little close when the movie starts. Poke it out when Juvenile comes on in the club. But don't be trying to hold hands, and be all kissing in Walmart, and trying to post on social media. We are not there yet. But we are at the point where you have the power to ask to meet their friends.

The old saying is, and will always be true. If you ain't met the friends, you know you're not important. Your first few link ups should be one-on-ones. Not everybody you meet, go out with, talk to, should, or needs to, meet your crew. Only the ones that you consider to be boyfriend/girlfriend potential need to meet the homies.

The reasoning for not introducing them to everyone is because you want your friends to take you seriously when you ask for their opinion. If you're always bringing people around, how will they differentiate who's special from who's not? Actions speak louder than words, so just telling them that you think this guy is the one is not enough when last week they saw you with a different guy. In addition, you want them to know when to give you real advice because you will need their approval. Plus, true friends are going to see

@esquedollar

things in this person that you may not, and before you go to realm 3, you want all the information you can get.

I'm not saying that they should decide who you date, but I will say that it is good practice to always get your true friend's/friends' opinion or endorsement before you start a relationship. Like we say in the Wolf Pack, "I'm with you at the altar, and I'll be with you at divorce court." A real friend is going to be with you no matter what, so you want to make sure that you get their support before making a commitment to one person. Who will you call when they piss you off? Your friends. So, if she is going to have to come pick you up in the middle of the night because you and him are fighting, then she should have some kind of say so beforehand.

Lastly, just because a man takes you out on a date, and treats you to a nice evening doesn't mean you owe him anything. Steve Harvey mentioned this in his book and I would like to echo that point. Your presence is payment enough. You being seen with him in public is payment enough. A man should feel honored to be in your presence, and the fact that he was able to do it by only paying for dinner and a movie should be seen as a bargain in his eyes. Do not feel guilty by going out on dates and never reaching for your wallet. You are the prize, and if he wants you, he will pay the price. And your future husband will do it with a smile on his face. Any man who doesn't feel like you're worth it, isn't worth you.

-Realm Progression-

Where we are in this realm is getting closer and discussing plans and goals in life. Finding out if the directions of our lives can merge. For example, I once dated a girl who told me that she didn't think I could function in her world. Meaning she thought I was too ghetto to be around her and her family. Which is exactly the sort of things you should be considering at this realm. If you want to go to law school in another state, and he has a job that he's been on for 5 years, and has no plans on leaving because he doesn't want to leave his mother alone in Florida, then dating might be where this stops. Although it is admirable for him to want to keep a close eye on Mom dukes, you ain't interested in her.

BF/GF = 60%

The first realm with an actual title. When you're together, and one of you is being introduced, it's no longer just, "Everyone, this is Jeff." Now it's "Everyone, this is my Boyfriend Jeff." Sounds more meaningful than just plain ole Jeff doesn't it?!?

Here is where the official, verbal agreement or commitment to be together is made. If you are here, then you are in a monogamous relationship with the other person. The discussion should have been very specific, and there shouldn't be any doubt as to what's going on. When the two of you hang up the phone, or leave each other's presence, you all need to be on the same page. It may sound something like this.

"Hey Becky. I've really enjoyed these last few months with you. Spending time with you, and getting to know you on a deeper level has been awesome. I believe I can see myself being with you in a committed relationship. And if you feel the same, how about we make this official?"

"You know what Shawquan. I really been liking you too, and I feel the same boo. So yeah, let's do dis thang and make it for real for real."

"That means that you my girl. I'm your man. And there is no one else, right?"

"Yaasss boo. YYAAASSSS!"

"And no more condoms...!!!???"

"Wait, What the fuck?"

Scratch that last line...

The two of you are a couple, an item... And as you can tell by the percentages being over 50%, it is clearly serious.

-Power & Responsibility-

The vast majority of people are engaging in premarital sex at this point. Sometimes even after church on Sundays (I couldn't resist). If you waited until this realm, then I'm proud of you. If you didn't, then I pray you're not at this realm because someone is pregnant. From the woman's standpoint, at least you were able to get a commitment before you gave it up. However, there is a new issue, at this realm sex is somewhat of a responsibility.

The whole point of being committed to someone is so that they aren't having sex with anyone else. That means that the two of you have a responsibility to satisfy each other's sexual needs. Now, do you have to open up the whole Karma Sutra book? No. Something needs to be saved for marriage. So, if you wanna hold out on giving head, you have that power. You are not her husband, and she is not your wife.

Also, for those of you who are waiting until marriage to start having sex, as long as this person understands that, then you have the right to expect them to refrain from having sex with anyone else. If they can't, then they need to state that beforehand so that you two can discuss some possible accommodations. Maybe frequent hands jobs, and fingers. Maybe oral activities. Whatever system y'all come up with, the expectation needs to be verbally expressed and agreed upon.

As for home visits. You now have the power to spend the night, but not the power to stay for as long as you want. An occasional night here and there is cool. But you don't get your own dresser drawer. You don't get to pop up at will. You damn sure as hell ain't moving in. And KILL YO SELF if you think you have the power to ask for a key. Bring a bag when you come. Take all your stuff when you leave. This is my place. Not Yours. Not Ours.

That "Not Ours" is serious. My stuff is still mine, and your stuff is still yours. Don't touch my stuff without asking. You cannot go through my dresser, my clothes, nor my phone for multiple reasons. The only thing that matters at this realm is that...It's Not Yours!

You have a responsibility to introduce me to any and everyone that we run into, or meet. Especially a human of the opposite sex. If I see you speaking to someone as I'm walking towards you, I have the power to ask you, or them, who they are and why are they here. If they walk away before I reach you, then you have the responsibility to let me know who that was before I ask. If you don't, then I will ask, and you gotta/better/have the responsibility to tell me. See how that works?

Another new responsibility that is changing could/should be your social media "marital" status, and adding at least 1 post with a picture of us. It doesn't have to be your profile picture, but folk need to know that you are no longer single. These dudes, and thirsty THOTS that're all in your DM need to be aware that there is someone of significance in your life.

The sharing of money can be introduced at this realm. Meaning that, up to this point, the man should have been taking care of all the dating expenses. When my wife and I were dating, we never went anywhere, or did anything that I wasn't prepared to pay for. Did she occasionally offer, yes she did, and I would say no thank you. It wasn't until we started our relationship, when we reached this realm, that I would accept her offers to pay.

Speaking of money...

Now that you and this person are in a relationship, one of the things you want to pay attention to is how this person handles their money. I say pay attention because you don't want to end up with someone, and y'all go broke because she can't handle having $2 above her lunch money. Plus, you don't have the power to tell them what to do with their funds. Thus, you observe and occasionally question for understanding. You wanna know how they think financially, how they view money, and how their thoughts align with yours.

With her power and responsibility increasing, my need to show I can handle everything financially decreased because now, we are starting a team. This is where she bought me my first gift. And this is where she purchased things for my mom's birthday. Before you get here, the man is courting you. It ain't supposed to be free, and it definitely ain't supposed to be cheap. It should be relative to what he can afford. He should be smart enough not to go broke for you, but be willing to prove to you that you're not just another girl.

One way to establish the seriousness of this realm is this: Here is where you have the responsibility of meeting the parents. In the previous realm you met their friends to get their approval before you started the relationship. Here, you're meeting the parents after the relationship has started, but before you ever think about moving to another realm.

Above all, this realm is where the real conversations about parenting should begin to take place. Becoming a parent is the 2nd most important thing you will do in your life. In that case, you need to make sure that, if being a parent is something you would like to do, then you and the other person are on the same page about most of the aspects of parenting.

The first thing is to find out if this person is even interested in having kids. No need to discuss parenting philosophies with someone that is not interested in ever becoming a parent. That would be a complete waste of time, but you may want to hear their reasoning for not wanting a kid. At the least, it will give you an idea of how they think.

Pause

In my first book I wrote about this, how I wasn't interested having kids for a long time. My wife said she didn't think we would ever go far because of how adamant I was about not having kids. But, time changes people, and now I can't wait to have a little spoiled brat and bougie daughter to drive my spoil brat and bougie wife crazy.

Unpause

Once that is established, then you want to discuss some of the important things about child rearing. Things like education, private vs public school, tattoos, piercings, child names, potential godparents, whether or not a stay at home parent is desired, how do you feel about the other person's family babysitting.

These are conversations that should come up and be discussed over time. You need to make sure that you understand the parenting views of this person before moving onto the next realm. How a person treats a child can ruin a marriage. Find this out before the next realm.

-Realm Progression-

If you're wondering why I have you meet the parents after the relationship, I'll explain. Just like the friends don't need to meet everyone, your family needs to meet even less. Only the ones with lifelong potential ever need to meet Mom and Dad. As a woman, the last thing you want is for your dad to be meeting 5 and 6 guys throughout your life. As a man, you don't wanna deal with the shit your mama is going to talk to you about if you keep bringing home different women, because eventually, while dad will say something to his daughter in private, mom is going to talk about her son and the girl in front of the girl.

Once the parents have been met, and everyone likes the new boyfriend or girlfriend, the relationship can begin to progress. The two of you start spending more time together and eventually you will start thinking about the next realm. It shouldn't happen fast. You should still be making sure that your life is set as an individual first. Certain things need to be in order before you agree to marry someone, or before you ask someone to marry you. You should be able to stand alone as an adult without this person. Your lifestyle should not depend on this person. You should still have your friends and be doing things separate from this person. Your relationship should not take you away from the rest of the world.

I always tell my wife that it's amazing how little she hears from her girlfriends once they get a man. That should not be the case. A relationship should enhance your life...not consume it. You should still have girl's night out, and girl trips. They won't happen as often, but they should not become non-existent because you got a man. It shouldn't take an act of god for a guy to be able to grab a beer with his buddies. Be careful of a situation where you notice you or your friends have become distant now that they have started a relationship. Aside from it being flat out unhealthy, that could be a sign of domestic violence.

Before anyone gets on any knee, the man must have that one-on-one conversation with the woman's father, or father figure, and parents. I met with my wife's father one-on-one first. Then, we went inside the house and I spoke with her mother and her sister. This is the MOST IMPORTANT thing a man has to do before proposing. Especially if the woman has a father in her life that has been there for her, and raised her. That dad is owed this moment. He earned it. If a man does it any other way then that is utter and complete disrespect, and disregard for the people who raised this young lady.

Plus, as a man who may be a father of a daughter one day, you would want the same respect. God forbid my daughter come home engaged to a dude that hasn't looked me in my eyes and asked for my permission. Over my dead body. He getting dropped on site. I may lose the fight, but he catching 1 quick chop to the throat, a cross to the face, and a uppercut to the stomach. And in that order.

Engaged = 80%

There are very few moments in life cooler than when someone proposes. I remember when I did it. I'd been practicing my speech for over 3 months. But once it started, and everyone in the restaurant began to stare, the speech went out the window and I have no idea what I said. But I do know that she said, yes. I placed the ring on her finger, and we were catapulted to a new realm.

My wife and I were engaged for all of about three hours before her friends started asking her for a wedding date. I, and luckily neither is my wife, am not someone who believes that the purpose of an engagement is just to plan the wedding. As you can/will see here, I think the engagement is a totally separate experience from the previous realm, and your last chance to leave before you get stuck for life.

Girlfriend was cool. It was cute. It really meant something, especially in high school. However, as an adult, relationships really aren't for real for real until you get to this realm. Here is where the two of you have made a decision that we are going to get married one day. Therefore, here is where you solidify your foundation to have a wonderful and successful marriage. I say it should last for at least a year before you even start planning the wedding.

-Power & Responsibility-

My wife and I moved in together shortly after we got engaged. It wasn't what we wanted to do, but I got evicted one random day, and had to find another place to live, so we just figured there was no time like the present.

Pause

I feel I gotta explain why I got evicted. I can't have y'all thinking the kid out here straight not paying his bills, but trying to help others with they life.

Long story short, my wife decided to go back to school for her RN degree, and she gave up her apartment to move in with her sister and became a full-time student. I was renting a townhouse from a lady that, unbeknownst to me, wasn't paying her mortgage, but was still collecting rent from me. I clearly didn't know this until I got this huge envelope in the mail from a mortgage company addressed to her. I opened it being nosy and found out she was 8 months behind on her mortgage, and I had been living there for 7. A week later I came home from work to a cop and 3 gentlemen with a big truck ready to throw all my stuff on the side of the road. But I got lucky, the female cop accidently placed the 3-day notice on the wrong door. So she taped it to my door and said I got 3 days and she'll be back. I called my fiancé, told her what happened, and we've been living together ever since.

Unpause

Cohabitating before marriage is a big decision. I, for one, am totally against living together if you are not engaged or married. I think a woman who lives with a man that has not formally committed to her and her family by putting his money where his mouth is, in the form of a diamond ring that will NOT be returned if they break up, is setting herself up for failure. Living with your boyfriend, and you two break up, the woman has nothing to show for it. At the very least, if you and your fiancé go y'all separate ways, you will have a few thousand dollars on your hand as some form of compensation. Even Oreos have a price ladies; which means that you need to put a value on your cookies too. Not to mention living with him could turn him into Captain Common Law, and you don't want that.

From the man's perspective, we are almost always interested in getting as much as we can while committing the least. In a cohabitating situation, I don't think it's a good idea because why give up your freedom if you're not ready to be married. Hold on as long as you can because once you give it up, it's gone forever.

I have a Man Law, in a situation where the two of you have decided on cohabitation, the man cannot move into the woman's place. That is just 100% unmanly. If the woman already has her own place, and it happens to be better than yours, then y'all start saving for something to purchase together. However, under no circumstances is it ok for a man to move into a woman's house. If he does, he might as well wear the engagement ring and take her last name once they get married.

This stage is the first stage where money starts to mix. The woman, now being your fiancé, has a responsibility to help financially, especially if she moves in with you. Also, while she always could if she wanted to, her ability to offer and help her man if she can, now becomes an expectation.

We all count people's pockets, and nowhere does it happen more than in a relationship. Part of the benefit of getting in a relationship, getting engaged, and getting married is to have someone to share the financial burdens of life with. As a result, when one is struggling, the other should offer to help, and this is the realm where that offer is expected to come. It's a team effort now, so if he's doing bad then so are you. Now, I'm not saying the two of you should have merged bank accounts at this point because that is not true. I'm just saying that money should begin to mix a little more. You should see a lot less "I", and a lot more of "We" when it comes to dollars.

-Realm Progression-

The wedding should not be discussed for the first 6 months of the engagement. Enjoy the new titles, enjoy the progress that you two have made. Don't be in such a rush to get to the next realm. But, at some point during the engagement the two of you will have to get to the business of planning the wedding.

This will be the first real/major test of how you work as a team. Being that neither one of you have been married before, (in most cases at least) no one has experience, but everyone has ideas. You are going to be involved in some discussions that can get very heated, especially because this will be the first time that you have spent REAL money together.

Pause

Our wedding ran us about $20k for everything. Some will skip the big wedding, and instead use that money as a down payment for your house. No one is right, and no one is wrong. It depends on what you and your future spouse want to do. My wife and I both wanted a traditional wedding. There hadn't been one in either of our families in forever. With neither one of us having kids, we figured why not do it big, and be a model for the young people in our families. A few people tried to talk us out of it, and a few times we talked about switching it up. But, 2 years later, our Teamwork made the Dream work, and the magic happened! I'm glad we did it, and I would do it all over again. Every day when I walk by our digital photo album with all the pictures from our wedding, I get a flash of a memory of one of the happiest days of our lives, and in the lives of our family and friends who were in attendance. So if you have the means, then I say go for it. You got the rest of your life to buy a house, but you only get married for the first time once.
#YOLO

Unpause

Use the wedding planning as a team building exercise. Don't rush it. Enjoy the back and forth conversations. The meetings with the different vendors. The trying on of dresses and suits. This should be an experience that you never forget, not one that you just can't wait until it's over. This will bring the two of you closer together, and make you excited about becoming one in the near future. Part of becoming one is the complete merging of lives, which means merging of finances.

With all the talk about money that happens with planning a wedding, or with cohabitating, this time becomes the perfect time to have the exchange about how you all are going to do your finances. Keeping in mind that sex and money are the 2 biggest reasons for divorce, this conversation is usually a sensitive topic, and needs to be had logically, not emotionally. But nonetheless, it needs to be had before you two move in together, and before the wedding.

Hopefully, the two of you have had the experience of living alone separately, so each of you will have some idea for how you will like the finances to be handled. Whether you're having this conversation because of wedding planning, or because you're contemplating moving in, it will go the same. Be sure to listen to the way the other one feels. In the great words of Big Worm, "Playing with my money, is like playing with my emotions." This means the conversation needs to be thorough, inclusive, and cover all bases. Some of the topics that will be discussed are:

How will we pay bills?

Where does income go?

Are we splitting bills?

Does all money go in the same account?

Are we getting allowances?

How do we purchase big things?

How do we save?

What about vacations?

What happens to big checks like income taxes?

What if my dad gives me a gift of $10k?

When Red and I had this conversation, I gave her my initial thoughts, and while at first, she was hesitant, she went along with it, and I can honestly say that money is the one thing we never have a problem with. My theory is this: all money goes into 1 account, we each get a weekly allowance to spend however we want, all bills and needs come out of the main account, all wants come out of your allowance. And if there is something big, which we defined "big" as anything in the 3-digit range, then we gotta talk first. I will give my wife some credit, she usually doesn't spend anything outside of groceries without letting me know. I really appreciate that. The worst financial thing someone can do in a marriage is check the account and see a large sum of money missing that they were unaware of.

Hiding money is something I don't believe in. As soon as it comes to light, and it always does, trust is out the window and the marriage is on its way to Unhappy Land, which is the first exit before Divorce Ville. So, make sure that is mentioned during these conversations. Go into the marriage with everything on the table.

Marriage = 100%

Ah yes, it's your wedding day. The last day of the rest of your life. She looks so beautiful in that white dress as she glides like an angel up the aisle towards you. The audience is filled with all of your family and friends. Your best man is in your ear saying, "I got the car running, now's your last chance bro." You smirk at him but never take your eyes off her. Before you can blink, "I do" and you're married. Your life will never be the same because your life is no longer yours alone.

If you have followed all of my advice up to this point, then you will be prepared for marriage because you will know what you're signing up for, and who you are signing up with. That's the 2-part approach to marriage that I stand by. Do not go into a marriage thinking this person is going to be something they're not. During one of our marriage counseling sessions, the counselor said that, "Men go into marriage hoping women won't change, and women go into it hoping the men will change. And the both of them are wrong." People are who they are; I don't care who you want them to be. And if you pay attention, they usually show you who they are early in the realms, whether you chose to see it or not is really the question. You have to know what you're signing up for. There shouldn't be any surprises at this point. If she gotta stank attitude, and don't like yo mama now, she will have a stank attitude and dislike yo mama in the future. Not saying people can't improve, but improve and change are different. I want to share something else the counselor said that is worth mentioning.

She asked my wife if she expects me to satisfy her every need, and my wife said yes. She then asked if I expected my wife to satisfy my every need, and I said no, "...that's impossible." The counselor said that in her over 20 years of marriage counseling, every woman has answered that question the same. And they all are wrong. No one person can satisfy you completely, that's what family and friends are for, to help where your spouse can't. Notice I said family and friends, not pool boys, and Side Pieces.

-Power & Responsibility-

Like when Jesus arose from the grave with all power in his hands, so does a fiancé emerge from under her vail as a wife with 100% of the power and responsibility. I remember when we closed on our first house. My wife asked the lady from the title company how long did we have to wait in order to refinance it so that she could get her name added to the house. The lady chuckled and said, "Its Mrs. Dollar right...???" My wife nodded in agreeance. With a heavy southern accent, she continued with, "Honey, you're his wife. Your name don't have to be on nothing, and it's still half yours." If there was ever a moment that described the power of a wife, that moment did it for me. But in case that wasn't a good enough example, and you still don't see the seriousness of marriage, here is a situation to consider.

If you become ill for some random reason, and are no longer coherent, your spouse is the one who will be making medical decisions for your life...

YOUR LIFE...

Not your parents...

Not your family...

Not your childhood friends...

If you get in a car accident and are rendered unconscious, and you don't have a living will, (if we're honest, most of us don't) your husband or wife is the one that decides what procedures they can do, and what medicines they're allowed to give you. Straight up. Your fiancé can get mad and post her ring on Craigslist. Your wife can end your life and pull the plug. That is what you call Power.

Wife can go through phones, cars, mail, clothes, bank statements, underwear, email, social media profiles, and anything else that you have if she's interested in seeing it. She can tell you that she wants you to fire that young secretary you just hired. She can tell you to stop drinking and lose 30 lbs. Why? Because she is your wife. Not to say that she should, and I hope that she actually doesn't, but if she wants to, she has that power. This means that if he asks for your phone, give it to them without question. Eventually, once they satisfy their insecurities a few times, they will get tired of asking and it will stop. Sometimes people just wanna flex their muscles, and that's ok. I would rather you allow them to exercise their snooping rights, than to allow them to think stuff because that's when they begin to think bad thoughts after bad thoughts, and we don't want a divorce to be the next thought in their head.

It would be a disservice to everyone if I didn't at the least mention divorce when we talk about the power of a spouse. This is the reason for all the foundational philosophies, the purpose of understanding everything I wrote in this book; to help you make the best possible marriage decision, so that it does not end in divorce. Getting divorced is another place where a spouse really gets to show off the power that the people in the lower realms don't get. At no other realm is the law involved in resolving the demise of your relationship. In the other realms, you have to handle it yourselves. Not the case when you're married and the two of you have decided to go your separate ways.

If you have never seen *Eddie Murphy Raw*, then you are missing out on the greatest divorce jokes ever made. "Half." Just the way he screamed the word half sends chills through me. So much so that I have been scared of divorce since before I even understood what marriage was. Just imagine having $2 and having to give someone that you don't like $1. That would make you mad as hell. Now imagine being married for 20 years, getting a divorce, and your wife being awarded half of your retirement. I once dated a girl who was going through a divorce. Her husband was retired military, and she was going to get half of his pension, child support, and still be on his insurance for the rest of his life.

Did you hear about the comedian Mike Epps' wife's divorce demands? Get ready for this. She wants $109k a month after 10 years of marriage. She claims that she's, "...too old to get a job!" She's 36. But it's not only women with the fuckery. This poor excuse of a man Kendu Issaca, Mary J. Blidge's soon to be ex-husband, is also asking for $100k a month. He says that he needs, "$5,000 a month to support his parents, $4,971 for two children from a past relationship, $1,200 on eating out, $60,000 in rent he owes to several properties, $2,500 on auto expenses and transportation, $5,708 for a housekeeper and maintenance on his properties, and another $1,723 on groceries. Please don't miss the part about the kids being from another relationship. What a douche!!!

With all that, it should be clear that there's a major difference in power for the spouse, and there should be. Especially when considering the responsibility that comes with it. Having access to all the bank accounts is an awesome thing. Therefore, it is only fair for there to be some awesome expectations in return. For example, while girlfriend might be able to get away with having a headache, wife is expected to roll over and make it happen. Likewise, when the man comes home tired from a long day's work, if his wife is feeling a little hot and bothered, then he has to find some energy to make it happen. I know people have to be understanding, but patience runs short when you're horny. As the husband or wife, you have an obligation to satisfy your spouse. Even if you don't do it at that moment, you need to somehow reassure them that you acknowledge their need, and you will handle it as soon as you get a quick nap. But trust that they will be sitting up waiting for you to wake up like a kid waiting on Christmas, and they ain't going to want to have to remind you. And they shouldn't have to. On another note, satisfaction does go beyond the bedroom, and it is just as important.

Coming home from work to the smell of food, a clean house, folded clothes, or things that a man believes his wife is supposed to do become the responsibility of that wife. Just like having a clean car, money in the bank, making sure the A/C is working, and the toilet isn't stopped up are typical responsibilities of the man. However, the two of you divide the chores up, there will be things that each of you are expected to do. Having a partner with responsibilities will help make life a little bit easier. Which is the point, right??? I once saw a quote that read, "Your wife should make your dick hard, not your life."

Aside from sex and chores, there is the responsibility to be supportive. I often say that it is not my job to tell my wife no, at most I will say not right now. Being married is about making each other better. Having someone to help you achieve your dreams. You do not have to agree with everything that your other half wants to do, but you should support them none the less. Whether you like the idea or not, you are expected to support them. Now, that does not mean that you can't or shouldn't express it if you don't agree, because you should. Be honest with them at all times. Nevertheless, you don't have to agree with someone's concept to support them. So, you state your disapproval, but you also ask how can you help, and offer your unwavering support.

#thoughtprovocations

The 5 realms will help you keep the status and progression of your relationships in order. The key is to know where you stand at all times, and to keep others in their place. Don't act like something you're not, and don't allow someone to treat you less, or more than what you are. Allow each realm to take its course so that you can optimize every experience at each level. Have patience and don't rush because you're tired of being lonely. I'd rather you take your time and do it right than rush and end up hurt, or worse, broke and hurt.

The break up with my first fiancé cost me thousands. It set me back about 2 or 3 years. As a result, I learned to take relationships more seriously. I can't get those years back. They are gone for good. It is important that you take every precaution before getting into a relationship and giving someone else your energy and time. While it may hurt to waste your energy on someone that doesn't/didn't deserve it, you can rejuvenate yourself and get that energy back and get those juices flowing again. But the last thing you want to do is be wasting the most precious thing of all. Time.

CHAPTER 6

ARE YOU READY?

I was scrolling through Facebook the other day when I saw a post from one of my old students that read something like, "Headed home...Do I start dinner for my husband or..." I didn't make it past the word husband before I stopped reading, and began commenting. I asked her, "When did you get married?" I couldn't believe she was married. She couldn't be a day over 22, and yet she responded that she had been married over a year already. My thoughts were, "What makes think you're ready to be a wife?"

Like seriously, those of you out there who want to be married, who are wondering why you're not already married, are you even ready for marriage? If you say that are you, my question then becomes this. What makes you be so sure?

For any job in the world, I think it is safe to say that the most valued trait in figuring out whether or not this person can do the job, or is ready for the job, is experience. I know someone has to be the first person a surgeon operates on, but who wants to be their Guinea pig? What experiences have a 21-year-old had that would make them think that they're ready to devote the rest of their life to someone else?

Pause

Any person who has heard me speak before has probably heard me say this; the two most important things we do in life, which are get married and become parents, are the two journeys that we embark on with the least amount of education. On top of that, it's the two things that we don't want anyone to tell us how to do. Why do we insist on OJT (On the Job Training) for things as important as marriage and parenting? HOW DOES THAT MAKE ANY DAMM SENSE???

Unpause

People need to understand what marriage is before they get into it. They need to have a clear understanding of what the rollercoaster can be like. They need to attend marriage counseling. They need to read books. They need to watch videos. They need to spend time talking to married couples whose lives they would like to emulate, and divorcees who they don't wanna be like. They need to prove to each other that they can do all the things that will be expected of them throughout the marriage. And before they do any of that, they need to know who they are.

The reason why a 20-year-old should not get married is because they have no idea who they are. Think about it. For those of you that are over 30, would you trust your 20-year-old self to make lifelong commitments? Hell Nah. Now don't get me wrong, at 20 I would have thought that I could. Clearly, I did, considering that I got engaged the first time at the ripe old age of 22. But at 34, ain't no way I would put my future in the hands of my 20-year-old self.

I'm sure there is someone reading this book thinking that they got married young and they are doing fine. Or their parents met in high school and have been together for 68 years. There are always exceptions to the rule, but we don't, and should not live/plan our life off of exceptions. We should live by the rule. Plan! Also, just look around...times have changed my friend. My grandma told me that she didn't get married at an early age because she wanted to, she did it because she ain't have nothing else to do. The average woman back then did not have the occupational options you women enjoy today. So, marriage seemed like a viable option as a "career choice," because that was the only way they could afford to live. Dual income was a necessity, and the best way to double your income was, and still is, to get married.

Today, people don't need a dual income to survive, but people still see marriage as one of the fastest ways to improve their financial situation. As sad as that may sound, the reason this person may be into you could have more to do with what your dollars can do for them, than what you do for them.

Prerequisites 1 – Live Alone

There are some things that you need to do before you decide to share the rest of your life with one person. Some are things that will prepare you to be a good spouse. Some are things that will help you to identify the right spouse for you. Some are things that will help you to be a good parent. Some of them are things that you need to do because once you get married you probably won't be able to do them. Most of them are meant for you to be more appreciative of having a husband or a wife.

Again, marriage is not about meeting the right person, it's about becoming the right person. Therefore, there are somethings you need to do before you get married. My number one thing is something that I spoke about earlier which is to live alone. Not just out of your parent's house, and not with a roommate. I mean 100% just you and some walls, and maybe a pet of some sort. Living alone will accomplish many different things, but the 2 that matter most to this conversation are you getting to know yourself, and you developing an understanding for what it really means to maintain a house.

Having someone living with you at all times, like a parent or best friend, will prevent you from seeing the realities of maintaining a house. Having to do all the grocery shopping, take the groceries out of the car, and put the groceries up, all while you just got off work, and have not eaten for hours because your lunch was cut short, is real. It is the day-to-day stuff, the life stuff that eats away at a marriage. Things like cleaning, cooking, washing clothes, paying bills, and doing the lawn are all things that become problems if someone doesn't know how to deal with them, or how to do them. What man wants a woman who's not somewhat domesticated? What woman wants a man who don't do a little cooking and cleaning and lawn work? What's the old saying? "I can do bad all by myself."

Living through these day-to-day deeds on your own provides you with experiences that you will take with you into your marriage, and those experiences will make you appreciate having someone at home that you can call and say, "Hey babe, can you come out and help me with the groceries."

Another part of living alone that's needed is the alone time. Not only will this help you appreciate having someone to keep you company, but it will also help you to get to know who you are, what you like, what you don't like, and what type of spouse you need in order to make you happy.

Being alone helps you to identify the aspects of life that matter to you the most. When I meet with a person who is having trouble identifying what they should be doing with their life, I always ask them, "If you had a magic wand, that would allow you to do anything you want to do, then what would you?" They often don't have a solid answer, which means that they don't know what they want.

When you live alone, you get to do what you wanna do, when you wanna do it, how you wanna do it, and who you wanna do it with. This is not something you can learn moving from yo mama house to ya man house. By living alone, you will be able to come and go as you please. This will allow you time and opportunity to explore the world and try new things, eat new things, see what's out there. As you discover the world you will realize your likes and dislikes, and become more certain of who you are, and what you want, and what you need.

Lastly, living alone before you get married will give you the strength and confidence to leave a bad situation. No matter what precautions we take, sometimes bad things happen to good people, and we could still end up in a bad relationship. The last thing I want you to do is to be stuck in an unsatisfying, or worse, an unhealthy marriage. If you were to ever find yourself deciding that you want to leave, you need to be able to leave. The truth of the matter is that some people can't leave because they are too scared of life alone, or life on their own. Most often, those are the people who have never done it before. You should be with someone because you want to be, not because you have to be.

Prerequisites 2 - Empty your Tank

My wife and I were driving down the street and a guy flew by us on his motorcycle. My wife shook her head and said, "I'm so glad we weren't talking when you had a bike. I couldn't be with a man who rode a motorcycle." Later on that month a guy passed us in a Polaris Sling Shot, I asked her if she would be cool with me getting one of those. She said that when I sign for it, I better be ready to sign divorce papers.

There are things that you will not be able to do once you get married. In your life, you have goals/desires/dreams. The person you're going to marry has goals/desires/dreams as well. When the two of you get together, those goals/desires/dreams are going to have to be merged in order for the relationship to thrive, and as we all know, in order for two things to merge, compromises have to be made. This means that you will have to make room on your bucket list for the things that they have on theirs. Plus, you will also have to flat out remove stuff, because your spouse won't stand for it. Imagine if I would have still had a motorcycle, my wife would have been down my throat about me getting rid of it ASAP.

So, if you think you're ready to get married, ask yourself this..."Have I done the things that I want to do that I may not be able to do once I get married?" Please do not forget the freaky, Rated R stuff that you wanna try. For example, the threesomes, sleeping with 3 different people in one day but not at the same time, visiting a swinger's club, do a money shot, certain positions, certain races, blood sisters or sorority sisters...(Your list may be different from what mine looked like, either way...don't judge me ☺) There is a possibility that you may end up marrying a person that is not down for some of the kinky things you like, or would have wanted to try. You are going to have to live with that. But first, you gotta know what you like.

Baskin Robins is famous for having 31 flavors because not everyone eats chocolate. We all do not like the same thing, but we all like something. The only way to get an accurate idea of what you like is to try some of the flavors. In order to look at another person and know that they can make you happy for life, you must have a very clear understanding of what you like, and how you like it. The only way to do that is to... DO THAT.

I'm not saying everyone needs to go out and sleep with a football team or the cheerleading squad. I'm saying that there is only one or two ways to handle this. Get married as a virgin, fight the temptation of curiosity, and operate under the auspices that you will never miss what you never had. Or sling that thang around a few places so that you have good and thorough knowledge of what pleases you. This is exactly why I can break down for you why I wanted to marry my wife.

I knew exactly the type of woman I needed, what she needed to be good at, what she needed to look like, and what I was willing to deal with. For example, I'm a very patient man who never loses his cool. This means that I knew I could handle my wife's _____ attitude. At the same time, I know that I have a very dominating presence, and I will run over a timid girl. I knew I needed a wife who is strong enough to check me. Otherwise, you will be roadkill under the wheels of my H2. Another example of knowing myself and what I needed comes from a girl I use to date. She was very nice and I could have been with her, but the truth is I didn't really find her that attractive and eventually I would have cheated. I have come to terms with my shallowness.

Knowing what you like is not only about sex, or sex appeal. It's is also about things like where you want to live. The sort of retirement life you have in mind. Whether or not you could deal with someone who travels for a living. Whether or not you need a person who cooks. If you can't handle, or just aren't interested in being a step parent. Could you be with someone of another race, or someone who believes in a different religion. The list literally can go on forever. You need to know as much about yourself as possible. When do you know enough? That is a good question, and I will try and answer it.

I knew that me, myself, and I were on the same page, and that I was ready for marriage when I was able to accurately predict how situations with women were going to go. Meaning I could precisely foresee whether or not I would get bored, if their company was good enough, whether or not I was going to be happy at the end of the date, sex, or phone call. When you can guess how you're going to feel about something, and you are guessing right, then you are no longer guessing, you know.

You must know who you are. You must know what you need from another person. You must know what you cannot accept. Notice I said know, not think. This is marriage. This is for the rest of your life. This should not be left up to chance. You need to know. Believing sounds good, but belief ain't knowledge; it ain't wisdom. And one can only have wisdom if they have done it before.

Prerequisites 3 – Why Do You Want to Get Married?

This is something you have to want to do. Marriage is no joke. It will be the greatest rollercoaster ride you ever get on. You will achieve an extreme feeling for every emotion there is, and that is of course positive and negative. You must ask yourself, "Why do I want to get married?"

When you do, say your answer out loud. Listen to it a few times. Then, tell a person or two. See what they think about your thoughts. I know people are going to be like, "Who cares what other people think?" Those people are stupid. Chances are you're only going to have this conversation with your closest people. And chances are, should you ever get married, these people are going to be the same people in your wedding, the same people you discuss your marriage with, etc. Therefore, their thoughts and opinions should matter.

The person who is going to be the one you call to get you out of trouble should have a say so in whether or not you get in trouble. Plus, explaining yourself to someone forces you to make sense of it, and sometimes, particularly when it comes to emotions, our thoughts aren't always logical. Ever thought something sounded good, and made perfect sense in your head? Then you went and shared the idea and the person you shared it with gave you that straight face emoji?

Now, the key is this, your answer has to be spoken without a particular person in mind.

Because if you do, then that's sort of like defining a word by using the word. That doesn't prove you really know what the word means.

This is your reason for why you want to be married, it shouldn't have anything to do with any particular person. Why you want to marry Amy, is a totally different conversation from why you wanna get married in the first place.

#thoughtprovocations

Before embarking on the voyage called love and marriage, I just want you to take a second and reflect to make sure that you know what you're getting into. I have a single homie that is dating this chick. They are getting closer and closer to each other, and beginning to talk about starting a real relationship. Every time he asks for my opinion I say the same thing, "Bro, you just gotta know what you signing up for, and know who you signing up with." There isn't anything better anyone can tell you than to know what you're getting yourself into, and to know who you're tag teaming with. This way, you are minimizing the surprises, and you can't complain, because you knew all of this before you said "yes."

Do not start something thinking this person is not going to be a little different in the future. You a fool if you do. Time changes all things and all people; therefore, you must know that they will change. How they change depends on your relationship, and the relationship depends on how the two of you work through those changes together, not separately.

Find out who you are, find out what it is you are signing up for by making sure you comprehend what marriage is, and find out who you're signing up with. If you can look yourself in the eye and say, beyond a shadow of a doubt, I know the answers to these questions, and when you explain these answers to others it sounds sound, then I would say that you, my dear friend, are ready.

CHAPTER – 7

SO WHAT, NOW WHAT

After analyzing all the different types of people, situations you can end up in, and ways to go about creating and developing a happy and healthy relationship, there are only two words left to say...Do Better.

Like I said in the beginning, no one likes that guy who points out all the problems and doesn't offer any solutions. To prove that I'm not that guy, I'm going to end the book by providing you all with some strategies for how to improve, and begin to see things changing for the better. I believe we all want to do better, but we sometimes just don't know where to begin.

First let's start with the ladies.

Women:

Whether you're the THOT, or Ms. Independent, the way to do better is the same.

It's all about balance, and being a well-rounded lady. As a woman looking to secure a husband, you must be able to hold his attention. Have you ever heard the quote? "Variety is the spice of life." As a professional educator, I can tell you that there are 2 main keys to holding someone's attention.

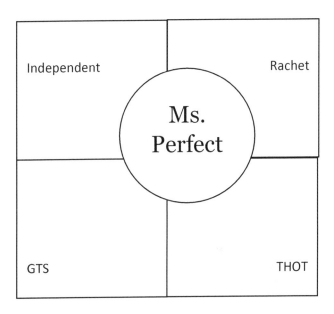

The 1st centers around knowing the person. This is why I said know what you're signing up for, and know who you're signing up with. You have to know them, the things that excite them, the things that make them happy, and be willing to do those things for the rest of your life. The 2nd has to do with your ability to provide them with variety. This means that Ms. Goody Two-Shoes needs to learn how to be a little bit like the Ratchet, and vice versa.

I explained how each type of woman has traits that men will like. Ideally, what a man wants is a mixture of all 4, with a slight edge going to one. If you look at the above visual I provided, you will see that Ms. Perfect has a good amount of all four of the women, but she is more Ratchet than any of them. You will have men like me who like Hood girls, so of course that is the main trait we're going to look for, but it is not the only trait that she can have if she wants to keep us. The same will go for guys who like Ms. Independent. The initial attraction will get their attention, but the mixture of The THOT, and Ms. Goody Two-Shoes all wrapped up in that Ms. Independent personality is what will make him want to stay with you. And hopefully marry you.

The man who runs the world does not run the world at all. The woman who can get the man who runs the world to do her bidding is the one who runs the world. She's the one who really has the power. Ladies, you have always had the power. A woman will always be the weakness of a man. It's been that way since Adam and Eve. Eve used her power. It's time that today's women use theirs.

Women could change the world in a manner of weeks if they ever got on the same page. But you all are too busy being petty and getting into cat fights over men...that you can't even realize y'all fighting over things that you all could and CAN control. I remember one of my students said to me, "Mr. Dollar, why do boys wear their pants around their waist?"

I turned to her and said, "Well sweetie, if girls didn't talk to dudes who did that, then dudes wouldn't do it."

Everything we do is to attract the attention of women. Why do we buy nice cars? Chicks dig dudes with nice cars? Why are we in the gym? Chicks dig dudes with 6 packs, and big arms? Why do we dress the way we do? Because we think that some girl is going to think we look fly and give us some play. Men are really simple.

Women lose because they compromise their standards for love and money. That is why a girl will deal with a cheating dude, because she loves him or he got money. That's why a girl will play the Side Piece, because she loves him or he has money. That is why a chick will stay with her husband but sleep with another man, because she loves one of them, and the other one has money. If women didn't sell their souls for love and money, then they would be able to get men to do better. Men are not going to improve for the sake of improving. Sorry, it will never happen. The majority of us will only do what we have to--the bare minimum! We will happily get that C and walk across the stage a few slots behind the person who got that A. And guess what, you still have to call the both of us Dr. Ain't that a bitch.

A happy medium is the goal. Not a total change in who you are as a person, but a few improvements here and there. Scale back on this, and increase in that. Do not change who you are for someone, but you can become a better version of you, that is the sweet spot.

Start by asking your friends what improvements they think you need to make in order to be a more balanced lady. I'm sure they will let you know where to begin. Then look in the mirror and ask yourself if those changes are ones that you're willing to make. There are aspects of me that I love, and I will not change. Then there are parts of me that I can see how they prevent me from being a better person, and those are the ones I work on. I suggest you do the same.

You will actually start to like the new you, and somewhere out there, there is a man that will be in love with this better you. He's out there watching you, waiting for those little improvements to begin to take shape. Once he sees them begin to become a part of who you are, then he will come and make you a half of who he is.

Men:

Now for the men. For those brothers out there who have yet to get married, I will tell you to take your time. Enjoy being the Playa, the Free Man, and Mr. Comfortable until you're tired of it, or until you meet a woman who is worth changing your life for. Marriage should be something you do once. That's why the girl is called the 1. So, you want to make sure that you are not going to feel like you are missing anything. I don't want you settling down and always be wishing you wouldn't have.

Also, just like I'm telling the women to use more discretion in choosing who they lay with, you need to do the same. Try to go into your marriage without a baby mama. That means to use a condom got damm it. Don't give me no bullshit about her being on the pill. Strap up bruh. You should be able to start a family with someone who will not have drama already built into the situation.

Lastly, make sure you pick the right woman. I don't care how shallow or stupid the things that matter to you are, they matter to you and don't have to make sense to anyone else. Be sure to know what they are, and to be able to recognize whether or not a lady will be able to satisfy and be that in which you need her to be. It doesn't matter how cool you think she is, if you know that she can't make you happy, then move on bruh. Marriage ain't something I want you guessing about, this is something you should know.

And I know that marriage is the greatest thing a man can do. Nothing makes you feel more satisfied and happy than a good woman to call your own. So, if you are not totally ready, but you believe in your heart for a particular girl to be worth it, then take a leap of faith. You can't hit the lotto if you never purchase a ticket.

The Last Word

Finally, the divorce rate is, give or take, around 50%, and half the people that are still married probably wish they weren't. Most of us don't personally know 3 couples that are happily married, or haven't dealt with some form of cheating, or beating within their relationship. And yet, everyday hundreds of people all over the world join hands and say, "I do." That is proof that we long for love, and we long for it to last forever.

It must be ingrained in us, deep down in our guts, in our souls to want to be loved, and to want to love on someone. So, go, find someone to love. Find someone that loves you, and love them back. In the words of Steve Harvey on Kings of Comedy,

"If you don't have love...
you really don't have shit!

Thank You for Reading

Currently available from
Mr. Esque Dollar

30 b4 30 (Amazon)

The World According to Dollar (iTunes)

Coming Soon

#YOLO - Real Reflections of Randomness,
Recklessness, & Romance

A Second Chance at Virginity

The Art of Work

Timothy the Zombie

The Boy who Lost his Smile

Sister vs Sister

Thought Provocations

Finding your Passion

Do Better

65363137R00130

Made in the USA
Middletown, DE
26 February 2018